P9-APU-002

WITHDRAWN

St. Louis Community
College

Library

5801 Wilson Avenue
St. Louis, Missouri 63110

the new jewelry
trends+traditions

PETER DORMER AND RALPH TURNER

the new jewelry
trends+traditions

with 231 illustrations, 115 in color

THAMES AND HUDSON

*Captions to photographs: where one figure only is given
this refers to the object's greatest dimension.*

Illustration Acknowledgments

Bachhofer, Joss *22, 23, 191*; Basen, Rien *13*; Carpenter, Ray p.12; Cripps,
David p.13, *11, 12, 48–9, 60, 64–5, 72, 80, 82, 96–7, 102, 111, 113, 121,
123–4, 126–9, 133, 152, 160, 163, 169*; Degen, Joël *20–1, 50–1, 83, 106–8,
112, 157*; Griebsch, John p.19 (Barry Merritt); Haartsen, Tom *14, 15, 90,
114*; Hanson, Bob *74*; Helen Drutt Gallery p. *27*, p.116, *19, 29–32, 36,
98–9, 127, 130–1, 134, 139–41, 156*; Hinrichs, Dieter *25*; Hogers/Versluys
135, 173, 178, 198; Kung, Johsel Nam *136, 138, 158*; Künzli, Otto p.25, *8,
28, 47, 59, 68–9, 144–7, 150, 164–8, 173*; Lüttge, Thomas *144, 154*;
Nieman, Julian p.12 (Gerda Flöckinger); Rickl, Veronika *16, 44, 53*; Sayer,
Phil *116, 179–80*; Schönborn, Philipp *153, 155*; Smith, Roger p.17;
Tschabold, Mario *26*; Ward, David p.15, p.147, p.150, *56–7, 61–2, 84–6,
88–9, 91, 93, 101, 103, 119–20, 159, 161, 171–2, 181–2, 185, 187–9, 196*;
Watkins, David *30, 117–18, 199*; Whiteside, George *190*

We also thank Aspects, British Crafts Centre, Crafts Council, *Crafts
Magazine*, Galerie Ra, Galerie Cada, Galerie Mattar, Helen Drutt Gallery.

*First published in the USA in 1985 by Thames and Hudson Inc.,
500 Fifth Avenue, New York, New York 10110*

Library of Congress Catalog Card Number 84-52518

Printed and bound in Japan

CONTENTS

Authors note

This book has been compiled by Peter Dormer and Ralph
Turner. The text, except for the introduction entitled *The
New Jewelry*, has been written by Peter Dormer.
Notwithstanding the inestimable guidance given by the
editorial advisers listed above the responsibility for the final
choice of material rests with the joint authors.

THE NEW JEWELRY
A Distinctive Signature

Jewelry is a decorative art and what matters is not the words that can be coined from it, but whether or not it gives pleasure to the wearer and spectator. Most of the works shown in this book are intended to do just that, although people who have not followed developments in jewelry may be surprised at the variety of design and materials now in use.

By the mid-1970s there was abundant evidence of new and exciting work in jewelry, as well as hundreds of art-school-trained professionals displaying considerable expertise – all very different from the situation twenty years earlier, when the number of innovative jewelers throughout Europe and America was small.

Today, we can see the fruits of a dazzling burgeoning of many kinds of ornament, to excite a wide variety of tastes. Some of the new makers have wanted success in the world of fashion, but others have aimed for recognition of a different kind from the world of art. The bid for art status has had several motivations – egotism may be one, but survival is another: art-conscious and design-aware people are more likely customers for the new jewelry. Most important of all, however, jewelers are engaged in a positive reaction against the sort of jewelry generally sold in shops and department stores throughout the Western world.

Most of the jewelry sold by large retailers is conservative in design, mainly because design is often the least important aspect of jewelry which is bought to celebrate or announce an event – an engagement, a wedding, a wedding anniversary. The principal consideration for people buying work for such occasions is that it should look ostentatiously impressive and expensive: this jewelry is a visible, tangible show of affection from one person to another. Much commercial jewelry is therefore designed within a narrow conception of what jewelry ought to look like. And ideas that were once fresh and lively have become clichés. In most commercial jewelry the design matters only as a vehicle for gemstones and precious materials.

Nevertheless, since the Second World War, many craftsmen and craftswomen, particularly in West Germany, have been working in precious materials and have sought to rescue their craft from clichés through good design. For example, the German goldsmith Hubertus von Skal explained his own commitment to goldsmithing by asking a question. Why did early cultures bother to decorate their pots? It was, he said, to give the pots emphasis and distinction, like a signature. And it is the distinctive and the remarkable that Von Skal strives for in his own work. What is curious about commercial jewelry, on the other hand, is its lack of distinctiveness – all the 'signatures' look alike.

West Germany has had an important influence on the development of jewelry. Here the work and teaching of several key masters – notably Hermann Jünger, Friedrich Becker and Reinhold Reiling – has formed the foundation. Jünger, a superb artist in metals, whose experience spans thirty years, has raised the aesthetic aspirations of jewelers whilst promoting high standards of workmanship. His position as Professor of Goldsmithing at the Academy of Fine Arts in Munich and his influential teaching have provided him with an impressive list of former pupils now working in Europe, Australia and America. Becker, from Düsseldorf, has since the 1950s researched into motion and jewelry; he is an expert in kinetic jewelry. Reinhold Reiling, who died in 1983, was professor in the jewelry department of the art school in Pforzheim. Pforzheim is the centre of the jewelry industry in Germany, and has been since the twelfth century. As well as having many workshops and small factories, the town has a unique museum recording the history of jewelry. This Schmuckmuseum (Jewelry Museum) has attracted many craftsmen from all over the world and had an important influence on jewelry in the 1960s and 1970s.

The early 1970s were an adventurous time. Two Germans, Gerd Rothmann and Claus Bury, and an Austrian, Fritz Maierhofer, contributed to an important exhibition in 1971 at the Electrum Gallery, London, which showed for the first time how acrylics could be used creatively. Since then acrylic has become popular with jeweler-designers for its many qualities. It is a rigid material, light, comfortable to wear and, above all, rich in colour. The 1971 exhibition also showed a use of imagery very much of its time, reflecting many of the stratagems of the Pop Art movement in painting.

Claus Bury, in particular, became a major influence, almost a cult figure, admired for his innovative ideas and skilled workmanship. He became fluent in English within a few months as a response to the many invitations he received to teach in England, North America and Australia. Bury's early work combined gold with coloured, translucent acrylic, but in 1975 he began experimenting with non-ferrous metals, eventually finding a way of enriching them with a rich colour palette.

Then he was invited to teach at the Bezalel Academy of Art in Jerusalem, where the desert landscape of light-and-dark contrasts inspired new works – a series of photographs taken of some desert 'sculptures' subsequently became the basis of three-dimensional metal 'drawings'. After these early experiments in Israel, however, it was clear that he would abandon jewelry, and since 1980 he has worked as a sculptor in the United States.

Naturally, there were other German-speaking jewelers whose work was influential in the 1970s, among them the Germans Rüdiger Lorenzen, Norbert Mürrle and Ulrike Bahrs, and the

Above, Ring on plinth. Fritz Maierhofer. Acrylic sheet, gold. 10 cm. Austria, 1973

Above right, First landscape project, Israel. Geometrical Formations, part 1. Claus Bury. Israel, 1975

Right, Diagonal. Claus Bury. Copper, silver, gold. 10.5 cm. West Germany, 1977

Austrians Waltrud Viehböck and Peter Skubic. More recently, serious German jewelers have begun to reconsider the assumptions underlying their work because of the intelligent, sceptical questioning of the Swiss-born jeweler Otto Künzli.

The most noticeable aspect of modern jewelry is the variety of materials used, and in this the Dutch influence has been significant. The history of achievement in modern Dutch jewelry falls into two parts: a highly inventive period from 1965 to the early 1970s, dominated by the rational, radical ware of Emmy van Leersum and Gijs Bakker; then, in 1974, the formation of the B.O.E. group, which rebelled against the rational aesthetic of these jewelers and tried for a freer style, B.O.E. being *Bond van obloerege edeelsmeden* – jewelers in revolt.

Emmy van Leersum and Gijs Bakker had a traditional training in goldsmithing, but both wanted to break with the past. In the mid-1960s, they designed and made a collection of collars and bracelets from aluminum. The use of this material had in part a practical basis, related to its lightness, relative malleability and strength; but it was also a deliberate social-aesthetic choice. The new work was first shown in 1965 at the Galerie Swart in Amsterdam and, the following year, at the Stedelijk Museum. Later in 1966 it transferred to the Ewan Phillips Gallery, London. Significantly, Van Leersum and Bakker have always had a practising interest in industrial design.

Above, Shoulder piece. Gijs Bakker. Blue anodized aluminum. 60 cm. Holland, 1967

Right, Experimental clothing. Emmy van Leersum and Gijs Bakker. Holland, 1971

Bakker in particular has concentrated on work in this field, rather than in jewelry, in recent years. And several young Dutch men and women who have worked in jewelry have followed his example – among them, Frans van Nieuwenborg, Martin Wegman, Marja Staajes and Maria Hees.

In 1969 the Van Leersum/Bakker 'movement' was consolidated in an exhibition in Eindhoven called *Objects to Wear*, which also included work by three other notable jewelry designers – Nicolaas van Beek, Françoise van den Bosch and Bernhard Lameris. One principle common to all was that the jewelry itself had minimal form: the human body became an important part of the jewelry and not just the thing on which it was hung.

In the early 1970s practically everyone in Dutch jewelry (with the exception of Robert Smit) espoused the Van Leersum/Bakker approach, but one woman, Marion Herbst, while acknowledging the achievements of that strong partnership, none the less recognized that there was an alternative. She began her own 'revolution' and formed B.O.E., a group which included Onno Boekhoudt, Françoise van den Bosch (despite, or perhaps because of, her earlier association with the *Objects to Wear* exhibition), Berend Peter and Karel Niehorster. B.O.E. was short-lived, but it succeeded in reacting against the dominant clinical approach. For a while the group, as well as other Dutch jewelers, looked towards Britain, where jewelry design was looser

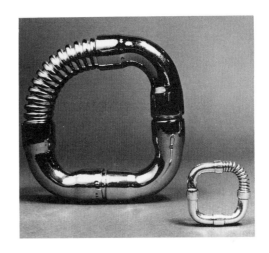

Bracelet and ring. Marion Herbst.
Chromium-plated copper. 18 cm,
3 cm. Holland, 1971

and freer. Indeed, throughout the 1970s there was a stimulating exchange of ideas between Dutch and British jewelers, with the work of, say, Caroline Broadhead (using tufted nylon and making structures from monofilament) inspiring the use of textiles and colour in Holland. Similarly, David Watkins and Susanna Heron, the British makers, were much impressed by the work of Van Leersum and Bakker.

Although B.O.E. itself did not survive, some of its members, including Herbst and Boekhoudt, have gone on being innovative and influential. Well-designed work, with a restrained expressiveness and colour, has been a characteristic in recent years of other Dutch makers, such as Joke Brakman and Willem Honing. A newcomer, Lam de Wolf, has also made an impact; like Marion Herbst in the 1970s, she may have opened up yet another set of possibilities.

It ought to be noted that many young jewelers, especially in Holland, Britain and the United States, chose to work in non-precious materials to make their work inexpensive. Other designer-jewelers, in the spirit of equality, opted for non-precious materials because they hated the values of wealth, status and power which they thought were wedded to gem-encrusted, precious-metal jewelry.

The extent to which the new jewelry flourishes in Britain is especially interesting. For most of the twentieth century, British jewelry has been overshadowed and influenced by styles and fashions created on the Continent and in Scandinavia. (A deep-rooted misconception still exists in the British public's mind that modern jewelry design stems exclusively from the Scandinavian countries. Undoubtedly the tradition of fine designs there, together with some extensive promotion, has impressed the British market. It is also true that Scandinavia took the lead in exploiting the design market of the 1950s and, as far as jewelry is concerned, the clean, uncluttered lines of Scandinavian work have had a lasting effect on many British makers.)

In the 1950s Gerda Flöckinger, an important designer, was the lone alternative hand in British jewelry. After 1961, when she was appointed head of a new experimental jewelry course at the Hornsey School of Art, the position began to change. Among Flöckinger's pupils have been David Poston and Charlotte de Syllas. Poston was an influential, socially aware jeweler of some significance in the early 1970s (and, as Chapter 1 shows, his work is entering a renewed period of innovation). Charlotte de Syllas follows no trend, but continues to make her own way, producing superbly crafted jewelry of great quality.

For a while, in the 1960s, the British taste was for rough, uncut crystals. Uncut stones are often the preserve of the amateur, but Helga Zahn (born in Germany), in her early work in Britain with pebbles and stones, brought a radical change to jewelry design. Her later pieces, employing agate, were among the most striking jewelry produced before the 1970s. And in an analogous field, another major talent of the period was Patricia Meyerowitz, whose work with machine off-cuts and industrial waste produced surprising and engaging results.

Not many jewelers at this time knew how to get the best out of precious stones, but Peter Hauffé was notable for producing designs that managed to enhance the character of the jewel. And, as a fan of Friedrich Becker, he was one of the few British jewelers to take kinetic jewelry seriously. However, the most successful British jeweler using precious materials imaginatively was Wendy Ramshaw, an important figure in the early 1970s. She remains a leading exponent of

Opposite
Left, Pendant. Patricia Meyerowitz. Silver. 14 cm. UK, 1965

Centre above, Necklace. Helga Zahn. Silver, black pebble. 18 cm.
UK, 1966

Centre below, Set of five gold rings. Wendy Ramshaw. Gold,
inlaid with red enamel. 3.5 cm. UK, 1971

Right, Rings. Gerda Flöckinger. Silver, gold, pearls, garnet. 3.5 cm.
UK, 1967, 1968

This page
Right, Necklace. David Poston. Limestone, hemp, mild steel,
cotton, bronze. 150 cm. UK, 1975

precious-metal jewelry whilst sometimes experimenting with alternative materials and
occasionally venturing into performance works.

The 1970s and early 1980s came gradually to be dominated by three names – Susanna Heron,
Caroline Broadhead and David Watkins – while a fourth individual – Pierre Degen – is now
contributing many new ideas to British jewelry. Others were innovatory, too, including Eric
Spiller, Gunilla Treen, Julia Manheim, Catherine Mannheim (who studied with Friedrich Becker),
Roger Morris and Tom Saddington.

Looking back, it can be seen that in Susanna Heron and Caroline Broadhead's work certain
key forms and ideas stand out as important markers in the development of new British jewelry
(although this is not to claim that they are exclusive to Britain). In 1976 Heron produced a
collection of acrylic perspex bangles which, for all their simplicity, had character and verve. In
1977 she presented what she called the Jubilee Neckpieces, followed by a range of perspex
works taking the theme of the curve, then by quadrangles playing with flat perspectives, by
flexible armpieces and by various 'clip on' works. The linking principle, paradoxically, is one of
symmetrical asymmetry. In the 1980s her work, with that of Caroline Broadhead and Julia
Manheim, developed into 'wearables'. In Heron's case these took the form of 'hats' which were
both expressionistic in their use of textiles or paper and minimal in their form – an Oriental
quality was now discernible. As Chapter 3 indicates, her work is no longer within the realm of

'jewelry' because her ideas are better realized as sculptures. Caroline Broadhead's inventions of bracelets and necklaces made with tufts of nylon held in a frame of boxwood were very influential – they combined elegance with practicality and simplicity. She too has developed a collection of wearables, some of which are intriguing and idiosyncratic.

David Watkins has digested all the formalist principles of De Stijl, but over a period has produced work which is very much his own – his pieces are often large, highly coloured metal drawings. Of especial interest in his work, and that of Broadhead, Manheim and Heron, is the deliberate designing out of all fastenings, clips and chains which would inhibit and impede the creation of a purist design aesthetic. In terms of abstract composition and colour harmony Watkins, like Eric Spiller, is one of Britain's most mature new jewelry designers.

The influences that have shaped the new jewelry in Europe, especially in Holland and Britain, and with notable contributions from Germany, Austria and Switzerland, have been healthy: a desire to avoid clichés in design; a desire to make exciting, robust and, where possible, cheap ornament; a desire to make jewelry that can be worn by either sex; a frequently expressed distaste for jewelry which is vulgar and merely status-seeking; and always an interest in ensuring that the ornament works with and complements the wearer's body.

It should be an obvious enough point that jewelry is for wearing, but perhaps not that obvious. In the United States, for example, the *current* tendency is to regard jewelry as mini-sculpture rather than wearable ornament which has to be worn in order to be seen properly. Considering again commercial jewelry, we see that much of it has been designed with no thought about how it will work with clothes or move with the body: all manner of objects, from butterflies to vintage cars, perch on lapels or dangle around necks. In Western Europe, by contrast, the major influence in new jewelry is the idea that it must work with the body – a principle that is itself central to the original thinking of Van Leersum and Bakker.

A demonstration of this 'working-with-the-body' doctrine in design can be seen in *The Jewelry Project* (1983) – a selection of modern European work put together by Susanna Heron and a British photographer, David Ward, for the New York collectors Sue and Malcolm Knapp. Some work by Dutch maker Lam de Wolf and Swiss jeweler Pierre Degen takes 'wearability' to 178, p.15 an extreme, and the non-precious materials used include nylon, rubber and polythene. Much of it, however, is discreet and designed to work quietly with the wearer – look, for example, at the pins by Joke Brakman. Such jewelry is designed for clothing and constitutes a simple, elegant 49 ornament which enhances the wearer without overwhelming her or him. It is the epitome of the West European modernist aesthetic, rooted in the German Bauhaus and the Dutch De Stijl, if, at some remove, influenced by the far older spirit of puritanism. Puritan or not, ornament such as this is as much at home on a conventional dress as it is on the tee- or even the hairshirt. Discreet, tasteful ornament can be worn anywhere.

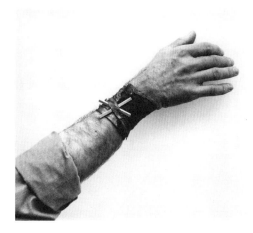

Left, Curved neckpiece. Susanna Heron. Acrylic. 18 cm. UK, 1977

Above, Armband. Pierre Degen. Cloth, wood. 8 cm. UK, 1981

In the development of contemporary European (and American) jewelry, certain individuals who were particularly influential in the 1960s and early 1970s took their initial stance from Bauhaus/De Stijl philosophy but modified it. Emile Souply (Belgium) is an example. Primarily a sculptor, he produced jewelry in the early 1960s that was grounded in Bauhaus teachings: the forms he made were vigorous and undecorated. By 1965 his work had become almost expressionist, making use of gold and baroque pearls. Although Souply is not, currently, a dominant figure in the new jewelry, his earlier work had much merit, not least because it was almost perversely in opposition to new trends.

In Czechoslovakia two important figures have emerged: Svatopluk Kasaly and Anton Cepka. Kasaly was especially innovative in the early 1970s – he used glass, a medium in which the Czechs are expert and creative. His forms are simple and pared down but, though it has something of Emmy van Leersum's rational aesthetic, the work is also warm – a quality it derives from its rhythmic aspect. Anton Cepka's jewelry from the early 1970s is severer and more sculptural. It displays a highly refined sense of colour and draws its imagery from such technology as radar and radio installations, which, as he says, have their own appeal and aesthetic.

In the United States rigorous or pared-down design is currently a less noticeable attribute than in Europe. And it is Americans who remark on the difference. Gary S. Griffin (American metalsmith and sculptor) said about the *International Jewelry Exhibition 1900–1980* (Vienna,

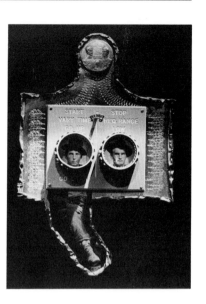

Left, Come Alive, You're in the Pepsi Generation. Brooch. Fred Woell. Copper, brass, steel, glass, photo, silver. 10 cm. USA, 1966

Right, Brothers. Brooch. Robert Ebendorf. Copper, brass, tin, engraved acrylic. 9 cm. USA, 1972

1981, organized by Peter Skubic): 'The European work appeared far more minimal than the American. It represented a design distillation process which resulted in a reductivist aesthetic. Good design and, in most cases, inventive design, [was] an end in itself in the European approach. This was significant when compared to American use of imagery or narrative. Here the hierarchy changed. The image became important; concept displaced the formal elements. The artist's personal philosophy was predominant, not predicated upon a design idea.' (*Metalsmith* magazine, Winter 1981)

In much American work there is a concern with jewelry as separate sculpture, and this strand of American jewelry history goes back to the ideas of the artist Alexander Calder, born in Philadelphia in 1898. Calder, the discoverer of the sculptural mobile, was producing moving constructions powered by motors as early as 1931, though he was soon to discard these mechanical aids to create mobiles which relied upon air currents.

Calder succeeded with jewelry where other painters and sculptors failed (so many have produced watered-down versions of the work they produce in the media that principally interest them). For a while jewelry was an important part of his work. With few tools and none of the apparatus of the conventional jeweler's workshop he handled beaten silver and copper wire with dexterity; spectacular necklaces, bracelets, hair combs and brooches came from his work bench and his first jewelry exhibition was held in late 1940 at the Willard Gallery, New York.

A year after this New York show, the Hungarian-born polymath Moholy-Nagy gave a tutorial at Chicago's School of Design. A jeweler, Margaret de Patta, attended and was very impressed by Moholy-Nagy's ideas. His influence and the Bauhaus philosophy became the core of her

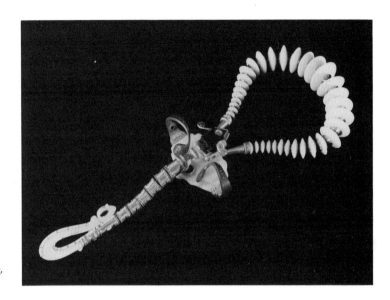

Pendant. Albert Paley. Silver, gold, bronze,
pearls, resin. 45 cm. USA, 1972/1973

aesthetic. And one of the significant suggestions she took up was his succinctly expressed exhortation to 'catch the stones in the air, make them float in space – don't enclose them.' An important figure in the prehistory of today's American jewelry, Margaret de Patta died in 1964 before her considerable achievements, especially in the use of the visual properties of gemstones, had been fully acknowledged.

The number of creative jewelers in America today is much greater than elsewhere and the pioneers of these jewelers are also numerous. Without the benefit of tradition or formal training, many jewelers in America learned as they worked, thereby discovering new approaches.

One of the most important trends in American jewelry has been the adoption of assemblage, interest in which was sharpened in 1961 by the exhibition *The Art of Assemblage* held at the Museum of Modern Art in New York. Assemblage in jewelry was anticipated by Sam Kramer, who in 1958 produced a surrealist pendant consisting of traditional materials, together with a yellow and black animal's eye acquired from a taxidermist and set in an ivory mount. Later, during the 1960s the main practitioner of assemblage was Fred Woell, who has relied extensively on found objects.

In the 1960s other influential American jewelers came to the fore or consolidated their positions, among them Arline Fisch, Marjorie Schick, Robert Ebendorf and Stanley Lechtzin. Lechtzin is a well-known goldsmith and one of the first American jewelers to experiment with electroforming. Now an internationally acknowledged master of the technique, he says: 'The control which I exercise over the metal as it grows in the electrolytic solution is a source of stimulation. This process is analogous to numerous growth processes observed in nature and has a considerable meaning to me.' The echo of naturalism, a preference for organic forms, is familiar territory for the crafts and for many people the essence of the wholesome, handmade, craft object, complete with thumb prints. Fortunately, Lechtzin's work is not too obvious or unsubtle in this respect.

Terms such as 'body sculpture', 'sculpture to wear' and 'body art' occur with some frequency in the history of modern American jewelry, notably in the work of Arline Fisch, Nilde Getty, Barry Merritt and Marci Zelmanoff. Although the main innovations in this field are *currently* occurring in Europe, the American Marjorie Schick is undoubtedly one of the most interesting contemporary practitioners of body sculpture. The reasons why body adornment has played such an important role in American jewelry is not clear, but the lack of tradition in conventional jewelry-making must have helped to make Americans receptive to aspects of jewelry not commonly practised. The influence of American Indian culture is one explanation given for the frequent use of feathers and other organic materials and forms. And, added to that, from the 1930s onwards the American experience, especially in New York, has been enriched by European émigrés bringing with them ideas and talents that were sometimes repressed in their homelands. It must also be said that the American talent and demand for spectacle and showmanship are forces much evident in American jewelry.

In much recent American work, there is also (as already noted) interest in jewelry as separate sculpture. Lloyd Herman, Director of the Renwick Gallery, Washington D.C., and organizer of the American exhibition *Good As Gold* (1981), observed: 'One might wonder why creative American jewelers working with the variety of materials evident in *Good As Gold* seem to limit themselves to brooches, necklaces and earrings.' And he provided his own answer. 'It is because brooches are pure form with very little need to function on or fit with the human body; they can be sculptural or decorative, standing alone without the aid of chains, hanging rings, or other fasteners which show and perhaps detract from the originality of their design.' Similarly, Herman went on, earrings and necklaces, although encumbered with chains and clasps, have the same sculptural possibilities of standing alone, but with the added ingredient of movement.

In some ways, the most striking demonstration of the gulf between American and European jewelry in general is Richard Mawdsley's 'Gothic' sculptural work. And yet Janet Koplos, writing in *American Craft* magazine, said, 'Mawdsley is committed to function. He produces pendants, pins and bracelets. One pendant that was too heavy to be worn demonstrates his determination about function: he converted it into a finial for the handle of a ladle.' The Mawdsley piece which has had the most publicity is the Feast Bracelet, an elaborate work which might be satisfactorily viewed as a separate sculpture, but which is in fact worn on the arm. Mawdsley's work is so dominating that the personality of the person who decides to wear one of his pieces is quite as interesting as that of the person who wears one of the *avant-garde* works seen in Chapter 3.

131

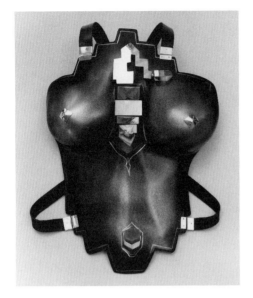

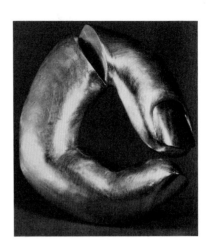

Left, Deco Queen. Torso piece. Barry Merritt. Fiberglass, silver, brass, bronze, leather, quartz, agate. 45 cm. USA, 1973

Right, Goldfinger. Bracelet. Bruno Martinazzi. Gold. 9 cm. Italy, 1973

We see a similar play off between jewelry and sculpture in Italy, where several of the important figures in postwar jewelry have been respected sculptors. This is typical of the Italian approach to design and visual aesthetics; their talented designers and artists are not inhibited by artificial barriers between disciplines. In 1967, for example, Gian Montebello began a unique workshop in Milan, inviting sculptors and painters of international standing to design jewelry in collaboration with the Gem Montebello Laboratory. After designs were approved, craftsmen made prototypes for the artists – including Max Ernst, César, Erte, Matta, Niki de Saint Phalle and Lucio Fontana – to approve and correct. Small editions were then made and sold.

Earlier, in the 1950s, the chief exponents of inventive jewelry in Italy were Anton Frühauf (pupil of the sculptor Marino Marini), Mario Pinton and the sculptors Gio and Arnaldo Pomodoro. During the 1960s the Pomodoro brothers were at the height of their inventiveness, with their jewelry and sculpture developing together. Their organic, naturalistic designs intrigued other jewelers in Europe and their influence was especially strong in Britain.

Since the late 1960s, Bruno Martinazzi, well known as a sculptor and jeweler, has used a limited range of images – usually parts of the human body – to create metaphors for various humanitarian ideas (see pls 142–3). His ornament is finely crafted, sensuous without being 47 pornographic. Like a very different, younger Italian jeweler, Giampaolo Babetto, he produces work that is both classical and chic.

37 In the linear jewelry of Italo Antico we can also see the sense of style, apparent ease of conception and flair which is so characteristic of Italian design. Antico is also an important minimalist artist, whose sculpture explores spatial and (through visual metaphor) temporal ideas

which are impossible to pursue in jewelry. Antico, like Martinazzi, Babetto and another interesting jeweler, Francesco Pavan, was active in the 1970s. The work of these makers promises to develop further, although it would be surprising if it followed the radical routes of some of the younger Dutch or British jewelers.

It is clear that the axis of this account, and of this book, is European-American. There is a reason for this, although it will be contested: on the whole, the new jewelry that is produced outside Western Europe and the United States is derivative from it. This state of affairs will not last for very much longer. Developments are taking place elsewhere. In Canada in 1983, for example, Prime Canadian Crafts Gallery in Toronto (run by Suzanne Greenaway) organized a radical exhibition called *Jewelry In Transition*, which was inspired by a London forerunner – *Jewelry Redefined*. Jewelers from all over Canada submitted work to this exhibition and Kai Chan, James 190 Evans and Richard Karpyshin, especially, were noted for their exciting alternatives to traditional 184 jewelry.

Australia's situation is not unlike Canada's: strong ties with Europe and a style of living in some ways reminiscent of the United States. The Crafts Board of the Australian Council has been particularly successful in establishing strong links with organizations in Britain and elsewhere in Europe, resulting in exchanges of exhibitions and special tours. In recent years Australian jewelry has come into its own, with fewer European influences and a greater sense of national identity. A new spirit is emerging that could have exciting repercussions internationally and new Australian jewelers well worth watching include Carlier Makigawa, Marian Hosking, Margaret West and Lyne Tune. Of course, the influences of European teaching continue, and examples of the European schools are to be seen in current Australian work. Hermann Jünger, Claus Bury, David Watkins and Wendy Ramshaw have been key figures and all of them have been visitors to Australia.

Japan is also taking jewelry very seriously, as the International Jewelry Exhibitions in Tokyo have shown. And Israel is producing jewelers of the stature of Esther Knobel. All things considered, it is likely that the European-American axis will move. To date, the new jewelry has had an adventurous time and the last ten years have been very exciting. Now there is a certain familiarity creeping into the work: clichés are not just the achilles heel of commercial jewelry. When someone does a critical survey of jewelry and ornament in the early 1990s, he or she will probably be looking enthusiastically at a much wider group of countries.

EXPRESSION AND DESIGN

Mainstream
Abstract Jewelry

Bracelet. Friedrich Becker. Steel. 8 cm. West Germany, 1980

EXPRESSION AND DESIGN
Mainstream Abstract Jewelry

What do we mean by 'mainstream'? Simply this: a glance through the pictures in this section should show that the work is familiar in its function even where the design and materials are novel. The jewelry is usually comfortable and practicable to wear, although clearly, in breaking away from the staleness of department-store ware, it breaches some conventions.

We have left figurative jewelry to the next chapter because its literal, storytelling content demands a different discussion. Here we are concentrating on the abstract and, without sinking too far into the sands of theory, discuss the relative merits of the work on the assumption that no good jewelry or ornament is arbitrary either in its conception or in its manufacture.

A broad distinction between European and American jewelry is drawn in the Introduction, but there are obvious national emphases which reflect differences in design interests and cultural taste within Europe (and, of course, within other countries mentioned in the book, such as Israel, Canada and Australia). Dutch and Swiss work, for example, is generally of a minimalist design: it has an air of puritanism which is not to be found in, say, Italian jewelry. And this holds even for the work by Giampaolo Babetto, the Italian jeweler who has taught at the Rietveld Academy in Amsterdam and has had a strong influence on some young Dutch jewelers. For all its reductivist design, Babetto's work has a measure of chicness which is not characteristic of other Rietveld teachers such as Onno Boekhoudt and Joke Brakman, both of whom are Dutch.

In Germany and Austria we see a greater tendency towards expressionism in jewelry, while the most consistently good British jewelers are design-orientated. Among those already mentioned in the Introduction are Caroline Broadhead and Eric Spiller, Broadhead tending to place an emphasis upon the design idea itself, while Spiller concentrates on the execution of an idea.

On the whole, the young European jewelers are not influenced by particular American makers, although the American contributions to abstract art and certain aspects of design, especially architecture, have been important general influences. Equally, some European jewelers have gone to study and work in America and have found the experience invigorating for their work – Joke van Ommen, from Holland, is a notable example. American jewelry is perhaps closest in spirit to German work in terms of its variety, its concern for technical virtuosity and its occasional hog-stomping brashness. American, German – and Australian –

jewelers are prepared to come down from the wall of obvious good taste (we all know that it is difficult to make De Stijl design look graceless, a fact which, on occasions, makes it a safe, boring option).

The new jewelry tends to fall into one of three categories. First, there is work which is expressive although still highly controlled. Such is the achievement of Hermann Jünger; Robin Quigley (USA); Suzan Rezac (a Swiss resident who trained and now works in the USA); Onno Boekhoudt; and Daniel Kruger (South Africa). The second category veers towards expressionism or exaggeration – it is work which not infrequently has a fetishistic or ritualistic quality about it. Examples here include Beatrix Mahlow (West Germany); Françoise Colpe (Belgium); Bruce Metcalf (USA); Marjorie Schick; and Annie Holdsworth (Australia). Their work does not, however, look alike. Finally, and by far the largest category, there is design-based jewelry. This is where one finds the pretty assemblages of shapes and patterns and where 'simple good taste' tends to rule. Some of the work, nevertheless, can be striking both in its technical virtuosity and in its suitability for a late twentieth-century technological society. Apart from the British jeweler, Eric Spiller, two good makers in the genre are David Tisdale (USA) and Joël Degen (French-born, but he has spent his time as a professional jeweler wholly in England).

It is not practical or necessary to discuss each of the jewelers whose work we have illustrated in this section, but it is right that we should draw out some of the key names. Hermann Jünger and Onno Boekhoudt are two of the most important modern jewelers in Europe, although they are not among the newest faces. The work of both men is expressive. Each manages to touch the emotions, as well as the mind, because his work has a spontaneity and naturalness about it which is akin to the best 'organic' abstract sculpture from the twentieth century, such as that by Brancusi or Moore – which is not to say Jünger or Boekhoudt are making sculptures.

Both men are influential teachers. Among the many important or promising jewelers taught by Jünger at the Munich Academy of Fine Arts have been Daniel Kruger, Miriam Sharlin (USA), Otto Künzli and Manfred Bischoff (West Germany). At the Rietveld Academy, Onno Boekhoudt has taught Joke Brakman, Willem Honing and Annelies Planteydt. All these jewelers we would regard as expressive, although each is different from the others.

1–4 Jünger's work begins with his watercolours and line drawings. The fluency of his drawings cannot be repeated in metal, but can be translated into it; the drawings are for discovering ideas and capturing a spontaneity which would be difficult to attain if all the exploratory work was done through making the jewelry itself. His development owes little to other jewelers, but a great deal to a German painter called Julius Bissier, whose fluid, almost Oriental compositions conveyed an emotional and mental attitude Jünger wanted in his own work.

Expressiveness in Jünger's work derives from two aspects of Bauhaus design – an inclination to keep design to essentials, whilst at the same time incorporating a freer and sometimes more playful ingredient, such as we see in a Paul Klee painting. This combination is also the foundation for other successful modern jewelers, including Robin Quigley. For Quigley also keeps her designs reduced and allows a playful and magical element (one deliberately reminiscent of Kandinsky) to come to the fore. 29–32

It is important that there is no attempt to force the design or the playfulness, thus emphasizing the importance of spontaneity. Spontaneity in this context is not random or uncontrolled gesture, but a fluency of expression which demands at least two ingredients – a skill, a dexterity, which is more or less second nature and is a natural tool to the maker's imagination; and a clear idea of where the design could go.

Jünger has a varied and extensive vocabulary of shapes and images, which has an affinity with both natural or found objects and with the ritual devices or tools of fifty centuries ago. In one sense his influence among younger German jewelers must be rather restrictive: since he has such a wide repertoire, his work offers rich pickings for plagiarists, and the young, having no voice of their own, tend to plagiarize. Yet Jünger is not alone in West Germany in the diversity of his work. Daniel Kruger is currently one of the most innovative of makers, and among the newest jewelers Manfred Bischoff, Justine Wein and others are finding their own voices.

Onno Boekhoudt's work is different. It is in the spirit of the De Stijl movement, but that is not quite the whole truth. The art historian Hans Jaffé pithily describes the secret of De Stijl as lying 'in the fundamental principle of its philosophy, in the concept of harmony and the suppression of individualism'. Harmony, yes – but lack of individualism is not a feature of Boekhoudt's work.

Boekhoudt's jewelry is not geometrical; it retains a natural quality which comes from keeping some of the attractiveness that worked metal has just before its edges and surfaces are finally honed up and polished. In his recent work, Boekhoudt has been making small collections of 5–6 objects in which only one item in each collection is to be worn; the other items are fetishistic, and so, by association, is the jewelry.

Simplicity does not preclude expressiveness. And the work of Boekhoudt's former students – such as Brakman, Planteydt and Honing – although simple in design, also has a rightness, a touch of fluent gesture that can be found in something like calligraphy, too. Willem Honing explains himself as follows:

> In my work it is important that the material will reveal itself in terms of what it is capable of doing. Perspex being translucent and opaque, papier-mâché being both flexible and stiff with a rough or smooth surface, and tar-paper being very pliable. However, it is not these material qualities which provide the starting-points for my jewelry. I begin with a certain feeling that I want to create and according to this feeling I arrange the elements which make the piece.

Simple expressiveness is not the preserve of Europeans. Robin Quigley aside, there are other Americans and American-trained jewelers, such as Miriam Sharlin and Suzan Rezac, whose

Brooches. Justine Wein. Silver. 6 cm (largest).
West Germany, 1981, 1982

10, 54   work is both expressive and discreet. Suzan Rezac's work is 'of its time', being an amalgam of metalsmithing skills and decorative devices adapted from twentieth-century abstract painting. The combination of such metals as silver, nickel, gold and copper gives her work a muted richness which goes well with the soft-edged geometry of the forms – a very touchable art. The overtures to abstract painting are seen elsewhere in American work, and the enamel brooches by Jamie Bennett, for example, are abstract 'paintings' made small.

    In considering the expressionist category it is worth noting that, almost perversely, reductivist design can sometimes enter the range of exaggerated gesture. An example of this is Gabriele

57   Dziuba's (West German) 'Z' pin. And there is also the work of the American maker, Marjorie Schick. Although we illustrate her work in Chapter 3, her more practical ornament has a place in mainstream simply because it is attractive and lively and, if on the large size, not so outrageous that it turns the wearer into a performance piece. She says, 'I consider my painted wood pieces as sculptural "stick" drawings to wear' and hopes that each piece, through the process of making, 'will retain an element of spontaneity and liveliness'. The work is expressionist

198   and has a tribal or ritual quality which, as we see in Chapter 3, gets taken to extremes.

    Expressionism usually takes more elaborate forms than it does in the work of Dziuba and

11, 12   Schick. Consider Beatrix Mahlow. The components of her jewelry – which is very finely made – resemble the artefacts found in ethnographical collections, such as axe heads, blades, tribal 'objects'. For most of us such ornaments and artefacts mean very little because we do not know their function or their context. Yet it is partly because of our ignorance that they encourage our curiosity, the more so if they are well made and interestingly decorated. Such qualities apply to Mahlow's work. Together with her materials – a combination of the metaphor-sustaining metals like gold and silver, and the translucent rigidity of plastic – it makes up a puzzling and frequently rather beautiful range of ornament. Consistent with the European 'tradition', Mahlow's work also takes on a new life and a coherence when it is worn.

Equally expressionist in a blunter, more direct way, is Friedrich Müller (West Germany), whose   26
simple brooches of twisted metal have more artifice about them than first meets the eye. He
explains that he is 'fascinated by the process which is imposed on materials' and what he has
done is simply to apply basic shaping to the bars of metal in order that 'the real value and the
actual nature of the metal may be divined'.

Expressionism in modern jewelry is a characteristic of American work. This is not surprising
given the nature of American design in daily life – in advertising, packaging and cars, and in
office and hotel lobbies. It is equally no surprise that the trend in architecture toward eclectic
decoration ('Post-Modernism' or 'Ornamentalism') is in its most interesting, exciting and
eccentric forms in the USA. One of the most lively commentators on American design – a man
who also pulls the rug out from under the arrogant feet of the European minimalist designers – is
Tom Wolfe. As he observes in *From Bauhaus to Our House*, this is the American century: 'This is
the century when America became the richest nation in all of history, with a wealth that reached
down to every level of the population. The energies and animal appetites and idle pleasures of
even the working classes – the very term now seemed antique – became enormous, lurid,
creamy, preposterous.'

Of course, Tom Wolfe's prose is lurid and creamy in its exaggeration and yet it rings
sufficiently true to explain why Holland and not the USA might be the home of 'quiet' jewelry.
Even the most basic geometrical work in America, such as Ann Scott's neckpieces, is bolder in its
geometry and patterning than anything in Europe which might remotely be considered as an
equivalent. Even where the work is really a matter of anodizing metals and shaping them into
bracelets, the American maker tends to want to express the geometry of the geometry.

These cultural influences have interesting consequences. We have already remarked on the
fact that America has had an impact on the Dutch maker Joke van Ommen, just as Miriam   74
Sharlin (USA) has been influenced by West German jewelers during her studies in Munich. Van
Ommen says: 'Although function is my starting point in my thinking, it is definitely not all. Of
course I want to make beautiful pieces as well. Lately a change has taken place in my work (due
to my move to Washington?) – it has become more three-dimensional. I experiment with
different materials, like mother of pearl, shells, ivory.' This change does not mean a change for
the worse in Van Ommen's work, though purists might cry for function and simplicity and might
gulp at the 'creamy' materials. It is, indeed, interesting that Van Ommen is responding to what is
an apparent feature in American design – the feeling that anything is permitted.

We might also argue that American work challenges a particular European orthodoxy that
development should be evolutionary, slow and rational. Who needs rational jewelry? Probably
not David LaPlantz, American jeweler and Art Professor at Humboldt State University,
California. LaPlantz is a success. Alan Revere, jewelry designer, has written: 'Praised by *The New*

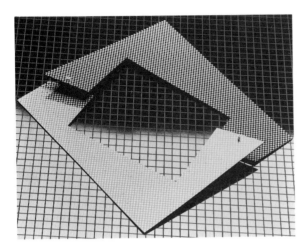

Neckpiece. Ann Scott. Acrylic, silver, steel.
22 × 22 × 2 cm. USA, 1982

70, 72   *York Times, Los Angeles Times* and *Ornament* Magazine, LaPlantz's new collection is a visual treasure chest. . . . The work is bold, vibrant, intriguing, and wearable. It represents the total commitment of a vital and exuberant artist . . . He has set out to retain the originality and uniqueness of his previous work [metal containers], however, and the jewelry is totally spontaneous. Perhaps a sketch or two, and then off he goes into the metal, to play out living dreams in anodized technicolor.' Currently, LaPlantz works in anodized or painted aluminum, creating vivid colours into which he engraves, so that the lines show through as silver. The works are constructions – 'miniature art forms' – and clearly stand on their own when not being worn. This is wearable art but not based on wearability. After two years of making jewelry proper (but after a longer period as a metalsmith), LaPlantz has work in most of the important public and private modern collections.

In one sense, LaPlantz is an epitome of an American ideal which manages to combine competitiveness, ambition, ego and energy with the belief that life should be lived with *wholesome* enjoyment – or, to quote from his statement of intent, 'I feel very lucky to be doing what I am doing both as an artist and teacher [twice voted at his University as its most Outstanding Professor of the Year] – both pay dividends that are worth more than gold – a satisfaction, a peace, a reason to smile and arise each dawn.' And although many European jewelers would sniffily dismiss all this as somehow not quite respectable or appropriate for the serious artist, there are others who would agree. Who needs an angst-ridden jeweler?

LaPlantz explains that his work is instinctive: 'I'm not aware of some of the things that are happening with the lines until after I am done. It's like you do the work and then afterwards say, well that's pretty nice.' He makes very few drawings and favours spontaneity, which is also a feature of his teaching: he gives his students problems that have to be solved within three hours.

'The decisions are not "can I or can't I", it's "yes", "no". It's like making a split-timing decision. If someone throws an axe at you, you have to do something. You have to respond. If it's wrong, it's wrong but then your next decision kind of corrects for that.'

The purpose of labouring LaPlantz's work and ideas is partly because of the rapid importance he appears to be achieving in the American modern jewelry world and partly because emphasis upon quickness, hard work and continuous change appears to be as much a feature of American work as caution and reductivism are among Europeans. There is certainly a critical distinction over the matter of spontaneity. LaPlantz's analogy of the hurled axe would not strike many teachers in German or Dutch art colleges as particularly appropriate. Much European art teaching is still very strongly rooted in the Bauhaus and especially in the spirit of the approach set out by the Swiss teacher, Johannes Itten. A brief paragraph, very much on the theme of spontaneity and taken from his book *Design and Form*, makes the point: 'A fern was studied for half an hour every morning during one week to grasp and understand the movements of its characteristic form. On the last day the fern pot was put aside, and the drawing was produced in a single emotion within fifteen minutes.'

The sort of spontaneity that LaPlantz epitomizes is different in kind from that of Jünger, Kruger, Quigley and the minimalist Europeans such as Johanna Hess-Dahm, Annelies Planteydt and Joke Brakman. They aspire more to the spontaneity found in Chinese calligraphy, where a stroke is quick and fluent but owes its spontaneity to a great deal of knowledge. Very few new jewelers worldwide have this ability.

A comparison can be made with expressionist painting, although it is a little misleading in the sense that there is little scope in LaPlantz's work, or that of any jeweler, for free gesture. Nevertheless, the quickness of design and manufacture, and the possibility of any one of several 'answers' being satisfactory, makes such a parallel tolerable. LaPlantz is an honest teacher and possibly a useful corrective to the unnecessarily rigid approach of some Europeans. He says, 'When answering a question, I will give at least five or six possible solutions to the problem in a piece. . . . So often teachers act like Gods with the one and only "true" answer.'

Work produced in this way may be attractive, but it is also true that such an approach is the dominant one in the second league of new jewelry throughout the West. The very best work has a look of 'necessity' about it – a suggestion that to alter the form or modify the decoration would be to make that piece weaker. One of the pitfalls of expressionism is its arbitrariness – and abstract expressionism, whether in jewelry, applied decoration to a building, sculpture or painting, may let you down, merely getting by through being tastefully random.

Expressionism of a different sort in American jewelry, one with obvious sculptural content, is apparent in Bruce Metcalf's work, which is more often table sculpture than wearable jewelry. 139–41 Metcalf has a wide vocabulary of forms and shapes which are largely organic, highly animated and very ambiguous. Even the abstract work somehow manages to suggest a succession of comic-strip cartoons. His pieces certainly entertain the mind because they are richly fetishistic, and all manner of scatological, sexual and violent references might emerge from these curious fantasies.

The ambition towards jewelry as sculpture, whether expressionist or not, usually takes one of the two forms outlined in the Introduction. There is the approach of makers such as Metcalf, in which the piece is seen as an autonomous object, and there is work which uses the person wearing it as a part of an overall body sculpture. Some makers try to do both. They try to make objects that can stand on their own as interesting autonomous artefacts and that also have another 'life' when worn: a difficult ambition to secure. David Selkirk (Western Australia) says that his recent 'solid pieces echo the form and line of the body but although fitting it sympathetically they have a presence independent of the body, functioning alone as objects'.

It is not hard to sympathize with the jeweler wanting to extend the expressive qualities of his or her work into the period when it is not worn – to treat it as sculpture, rather than a fashion accessory spending most of its time in a drawer. But really rather little of the jewelry that is designed to have a separate aesthetic life is worthy of the title 'sculpture'; it belongs more readily to the category of domestic ornament – the category occupied by most ceramic- and glassware, with its function being to decorate and to distract. (Arguably, a lot of work that is called 'sculpture' is in the same category.) This implies a constraint – one resented by more ambitious makers – for jewelry to be well mannered, deferring to the fact that it is to be worn by someone or live in someone's house. What suits the gallery need not suit the function of personal adornment and domestic decoration. At the same time, if the point of testing limitations is in fact to make more interesting, innovative and wearable work, then such questioning is not only healthy but necessary. One consistently thoughtful jeweler in this regard is David Watkins. His work has progressed naturally over a ten-year period, marked always by very fine craftsmanship and an excellent sense of colour. During this decade he has taken excursions into body sculpture and the results have fed back into his functional ware. In other words, he has not fallen to the temptation to make arbitrary, large-scale performance pieces just for the sake of being different. In many respects, his new geometrical work, whilst it is clearly unconventional, is none the less well within any recognized definition and practice of jewelry.

Makers do talk about their work 'making a statement', but they have borrowed the jargon from fine artists, most of whom are equally at a loss, if pressed, to indicate what the content of such a statement might mean. Notwithstanding its expressive and expressionist capacities, most of the new jewelry is simple design, though not necessarily the worse for that.

To devise ornament and design that will stay fresh is clearly difficult, especially since staying fresh is not to be confused with fashion. Much good ornament from the Arts and Crafts

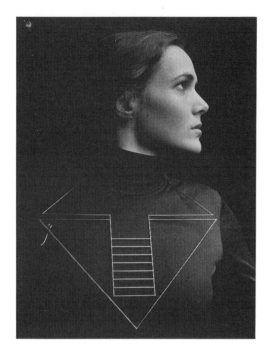

Double triangle. Neckpiece. David Watkins.
Steel, with yellow gold. 45 cm. UK, 1978

Movement, Jugendstil, Art Nouveau and Art Deco has passed in and out of fashion, but has always been recognized as good ornament. Indeed, the rapidity with which 'movements' are rediscovered might make one suspect that the last decade has not been a fertile period for inventive ornament. We think otherwise. There has certainly been some purely 'design'-based new jewelry which has a perfection of pattern about it which makes it continuously pleasing. Such work tends not to 'express' anything other than how it is to be worn, and mostly not even that: it simply 'is'. People to single out here include Eric Spiller, Caroline Broadhead, Paul Derrez (Holland), Nora Fok (Hong Kong), Therese Hilbert (Switzerland), Frank Bauer (West Germany), Jean-Paul Aleman (France), Joël Degen and David Tisdale.

Their work is demonstrably clever. Caroline Broadhead's idea of simply pushing one's hand (or head) through tufts of coloured nylon or cotton was almost laughably simple, but it has produced ornament which is both elegant and pretty. Mecky van den Brink's jewelry at the beginning of the 1980s is a good example of the Broadhead influence, as is Nora Fok's. Nora Fok, however, prefers to use colour and form with delicacy and restraint.   101

Paul Derrez's work also has about it a quality of reserve – it is rational design without being inhuman, and, like quite a lot of Dutch work, is reminiscent of traditional Dutch dress; his 'neckpieces' have as their antecedents the beautiful, large ruffs of 17th-century Dutch dress. Derrez, commenting on why he had selected a particular work for the *Jewelry Redefined* show in   120

London (1982), gave an explanation of his own values in jewelry. 'For me this piece is original, humorous and clever. It has logical shape which shows how to fasten it. The opposing materials give it a powerful contrast, and both men and women can wear it without any connotations of luxury, wealth and status. This is exactly my approach to jewelry.'

Making work that is properly of its own time is not so easy. We know that this is the age of technology and that the best craftsmanship and design is to be found in the aircraft, space and communications industries. Yet a straightforward lifting of technological imagery would not lead to good ornament. On the other hand, if the spirit of technology's perfection can be taken as a starting point, then the results can be very good. Eric Spiller's work is an example. Much of it is not simple; it has been mathematically worked out and meticulously executed and machine-tooled. Nothing is left to chance. But an element of that precious 'spontaneity', which has surfaced so many times in this chapter, is present because he makes use of chance-effects of light as the object moves when it is worn. Edward de Large, who was born in Britain but lives in the USA, also captures the spirit of technology and he has had an important influence in America through his research into anodizing titanium.

Some design-based jewelry takes its cue from expressing its function and this is a feature of David Tisdale's work. Tisdale's work is characteristically American in that it can stand on its own as autonomous ornament, unlike (for example) the much simpler work of the Dutch jeweler, Coen Mulder, which is otherwise similar in materials and function. Mulder's work comes alive only when worn. And Tisdale is almost expressionistic in making his design speak its function. His bangle, for example, exaggerates the function of enclosing the wrist into a piece of engineering; its construction has been strongly emphasized.

Frank Bauer is one who lies between the soft-edge designers, such as Broadhead and Fok, and the machine-aesthetic designers, such as Spiller and Tisdale. Bauer has moved on from his beautifully made intricate gold structures (mostly pendants and brooches) to pins with rubber thread. These are very simple and cling to the clothing like burrs: an elegant design.

The only constraints on design in new jewelry are straightforward practical ones and even these can be broken if wearers can be persuaded to co-operate. Yet there have been surprisingly few adventures outside geometry. In the figurative section, there are some innovative designs from, for example, Manfred Bischoff, but the new jewelers in Europe tend to keep their designs controlled and plain. There is, perhaps, a lack of confidence among most of the younger jewelers in making patterns.

In one way the new jewelers have spared themselves the effort and the need for 'decorating' their work because their materials frequently offer a range of colours and abstract patterns built in. For example, there is a variety of plastics which are manufactured in order to catch the light and break it into rainbow colours; there are also many different kinds of foil, coloured yarns and coated papers which are inherently pretty and well suited to the 'cut and fold' geometries favoured by many of the younger jewelers. It is almost tempting to say that the alternative materials have been less flexible in some respects than the traditional ones. For where there is a need to beat, hammer and forge there also develops the desire to experiment and force the material to its limits. This is the route to surprise. On the other hand, when the limitations of the material are apparent and the colour and even the pattern are 'given', then cutting and folding is all that is left: innovation is dependent only upon novel assemblage techniques.

Sometimes what is missed is the pleasure of good workmanship. All design and ornament can be undermined by bad workmanship, as we know. But there have been occasions during the last ten years or so when it has been fashionable to set 'craft' on one side on the assumption that 'craft' is boring and plodding and somehow prevents the Phoenix of creativity from rising. What has happened is that the Phoenix has turned into an Icarus. Workmanship has been treated with disdain in some quarters as though it were an attribute which anyone could easily attain for themselves. The most familiar attack on craftsmanship has been that an overemphasis on technique kills the spontaneity of a design. Certainly an overworking of materials can damage the look of an object; it is possible to over-polish, overdo the crispness of an edge, dull a colour or have an altogether over-finished look to a design. But overworking is bad craftsmanship. We are concerned with appropriate workmanship. David Poston, the British jeweler, has decided in his 121 new work that the design requires a certain looseness of finish, he wants to retain a flavour of what the metal looks like when it is being worked. This is good. It is not carelessness; it is not a matter of whamming something together for a quick effect.

Good workmanship has to be as much a feature of working non-precious metals as it is of gold and silver. In some cases there has been a laxness about quality, but the trend is currently firmly against this – it is a part of the spirit of the 1980s that a concern for quality of manufacture and design is uppermost in the purchaser's, as well as the maker's, mind.

Opposite
1 Pendants and brooch
   Hermann Jünger
   Gold, silver
   4–10 cm
   West Germany, 1980

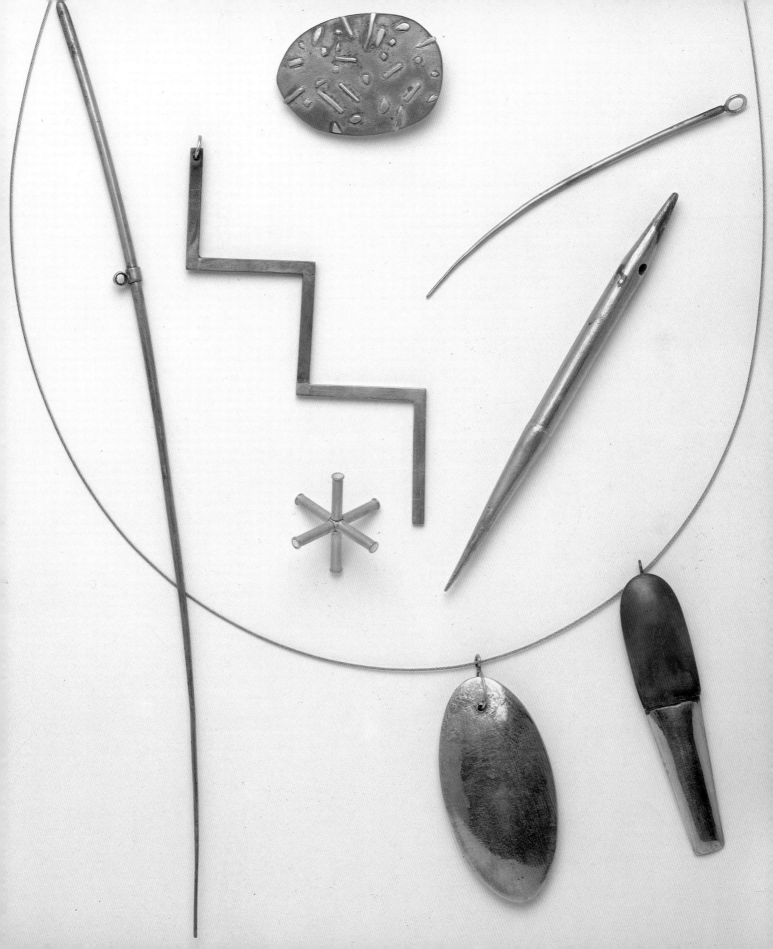

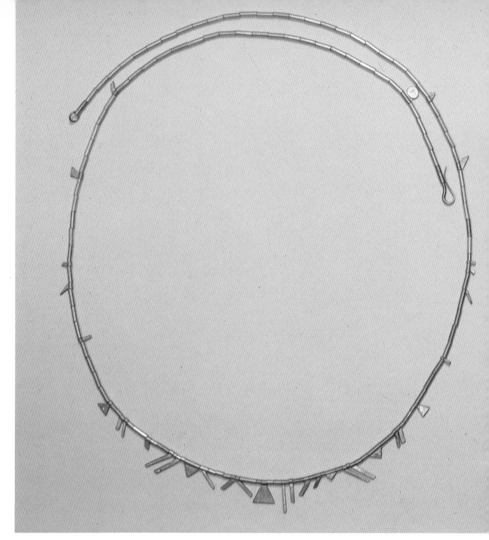

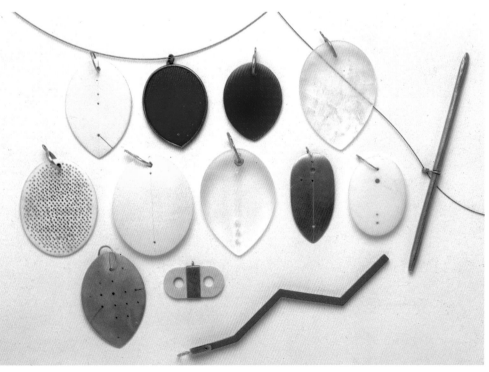

2 Two necklaces
   Hermann Jünger
   Gold, silver
   60 cm, 50 cm
   West Germany, 1980

3 Pendants
   Hermann Jünger
   Gold, silver, enamel
   4.5–14.5 cm
   West Germany, 1978, 1979

4 Pendants
   Hermann Jünger
   Gold, silver, agates
   7 cm
   West Germany, 1981

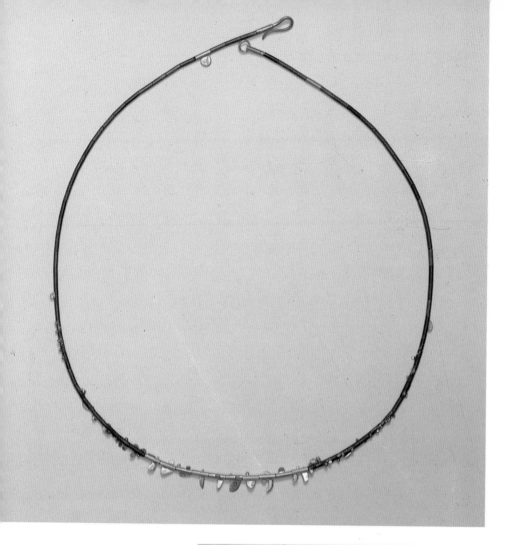

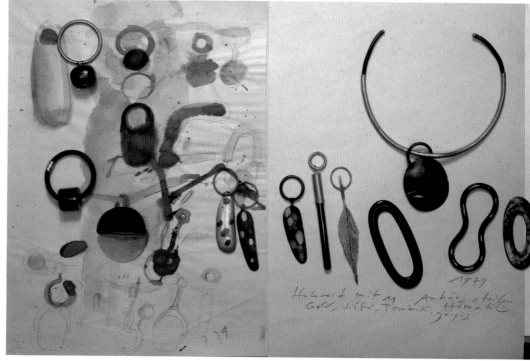

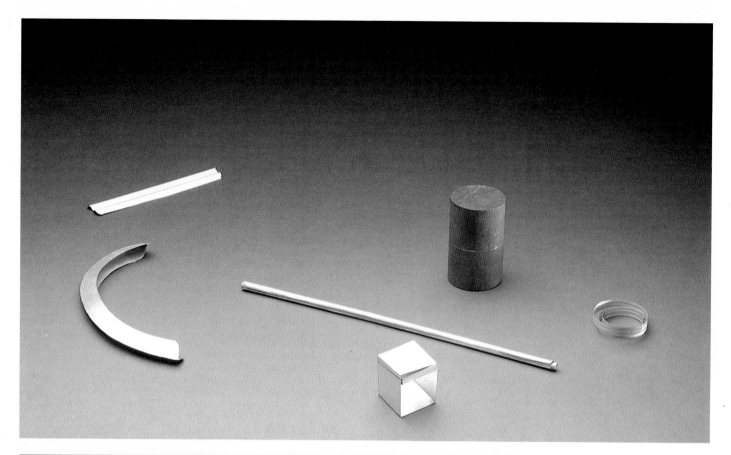

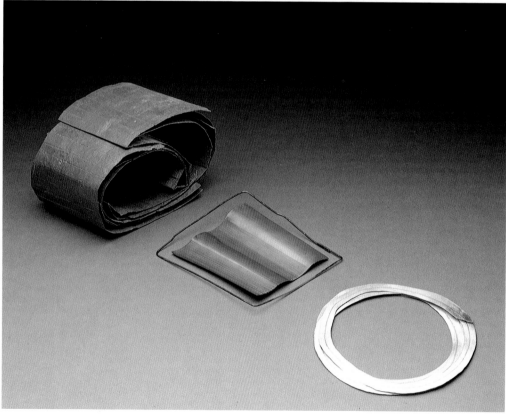

5 Rings with objects
  Onno Boekhoudt
  Silver, copper, steel
  2–10 cm
  Holland, 1983

6 Armband with objects
  Onno Boekhoudt
  Silver, copper, lead
  10 cm
  Holland, 1983

7 Necklace, earrings
  Daniel Kruger
  Silver
  18 cm d, 4 cm d
  West Germany, 1983

8 Necklace
  Daniel Kruger
  Silver, thread, glass beads
  18 cm d
  West Germany, 1975

9 Two brooches
  Miriam Sharlin
  Silver, copper, stainless steel
  8 × 7 cm
  USA, 1982

10 Bracelet
   Suzan Rezac
   Silver
   11 cm
   USA, 1983

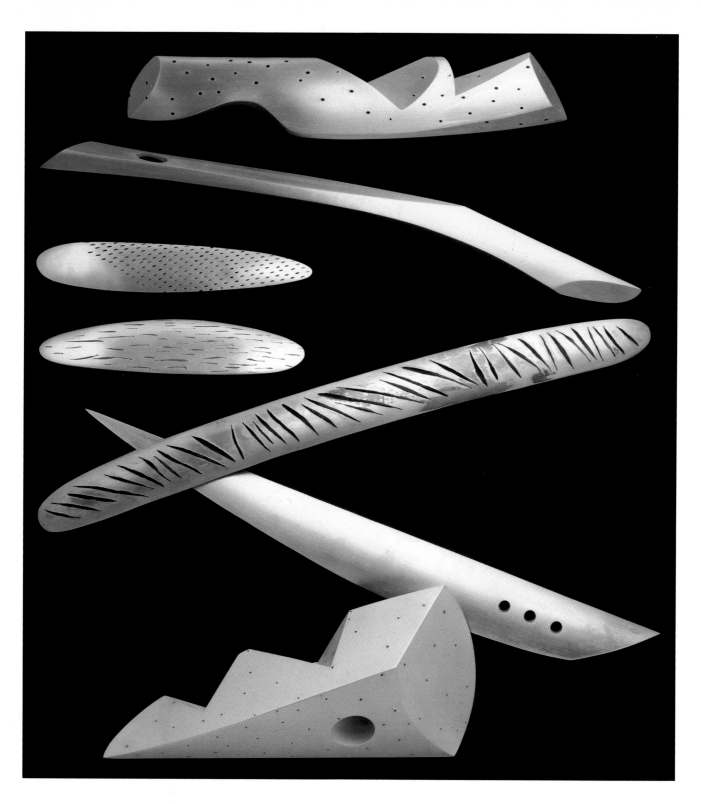

11 Wearable objects/pendants
   Beatrix Mahlow
   Silver, gold-coloured metals
   12–24 cm
   UK/West Germany, 1982

12 Neckpiece
   Beatrix Mahlow
   Painted metal, etched acrylic
   24 cm
   UK/West Germany, 1982

13 Bracelet
   Gijs Bakker
   Aluminum
   9 cm
   Holland, 1968

14 Bracelet for
   the upper arm
   Willem Honing
   Sawn perspex
   10.4 cm
   Holland, 1981

15 Bracelet for
   the upper arm
   Willem Honing
   Sawn perspex
   14 cm
   Holland, 1981

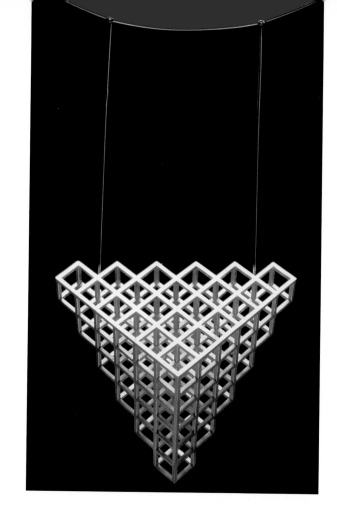

16 Pins
   Rita Grosse-Ruyken
   Forged gold
   22 × 9 cm
   West Germany, 1977

17 Pendant
   Frank Bauer
   Gold
   20 cm h
   West Germany/UK, 1980

18 Necklace
   Annelies Planteydt
   Gold
   15 cm
   Holland, 1983

19 Necklace
   Caroline Strieb
   Gold, ivory
   15 cm
   USA, 1983

20 Earrings
   Holly Belsher
   Gilding metal, steel
   5 cm h
   UK, 1981

21 Earrings
   Cornelia Ratting
   Gold, steel
   5 × 3.5 cm
   UK, 1982

22, 23
Brooches
Jan Wehrens
Gold
5 cm, 10 cm
West Germany, 1980, 1981

24 Set of four pins
Wendy Ramshaw
Gold, black basalt,
    opal, moonstone
12, 14, 12, 14 cm
UK, 1981

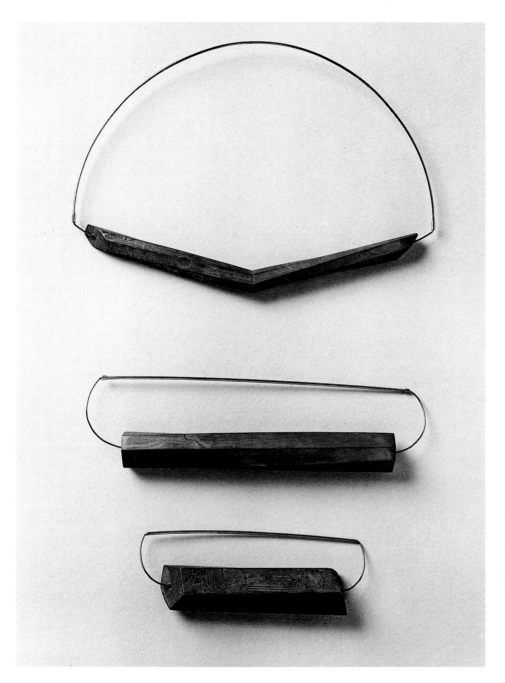

25 Three brooches
  Doris Sacher
  Gold, silver
  14 cm
  West Germany, 1981

26 Brooch
  Friedrich Müller
  Brass, steel
  7 cm
  West Germany, 1982

27 Bracelet
  Annette Rössle
  Copper, gold
  12 cm
  West Germany, 1978

28 Bracelet
  Daniel Kruger
  Silver
  7 cm
  West Germany, 1982

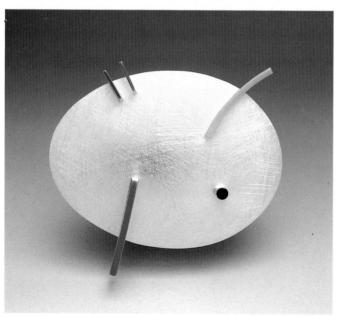
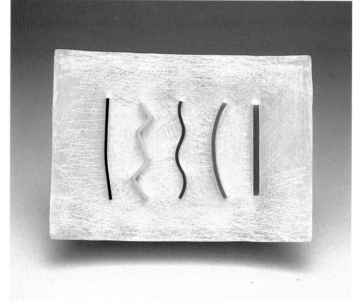

29–32
Four brooches
Robin Quigley
Silver, epoxy resin
6.25 cm
USA, 1982

33 Bracelet
Annie Holdsworth
Acrylic, silver
9 cm
Australia, 1982

34 Brooch
   Jamie Bennett
   Enamel, silver
   5 cm
   USA, 1979

35 Rectangular pattern bracelet
   David Tisdale
   Anodized aluminum, silver, onyx
   7 × 3 × 5.5 cm
   USA, 1983

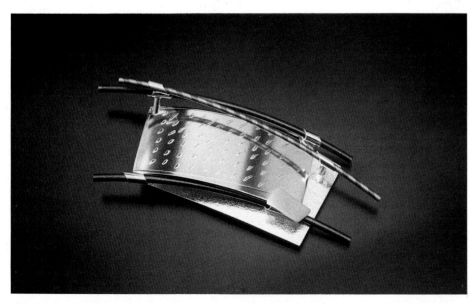

36 Brooch
   Helen Shirk
   Silver, titanium, gold
   7.5 cm
   USA, 1982

37 Necklace
   Italo Antico
   Silver
   32 cm
   Italy, 1976

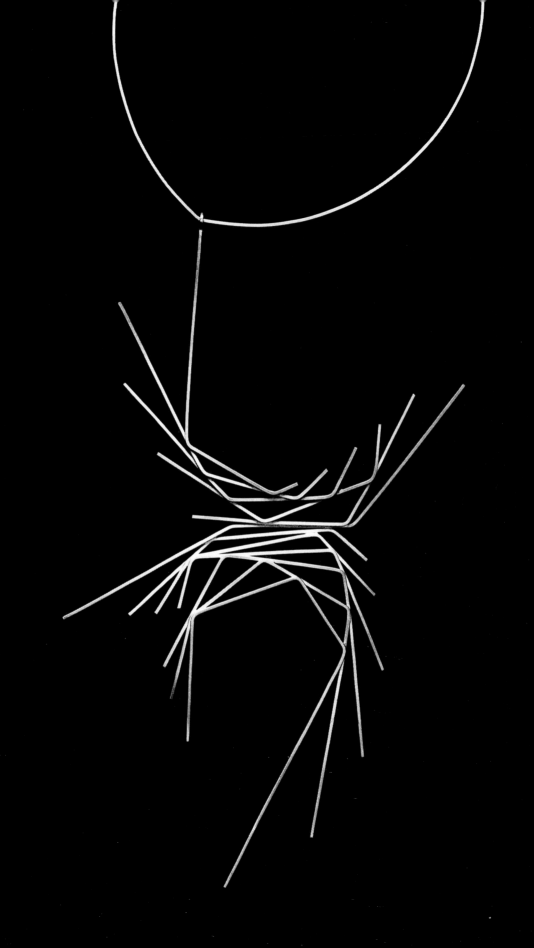

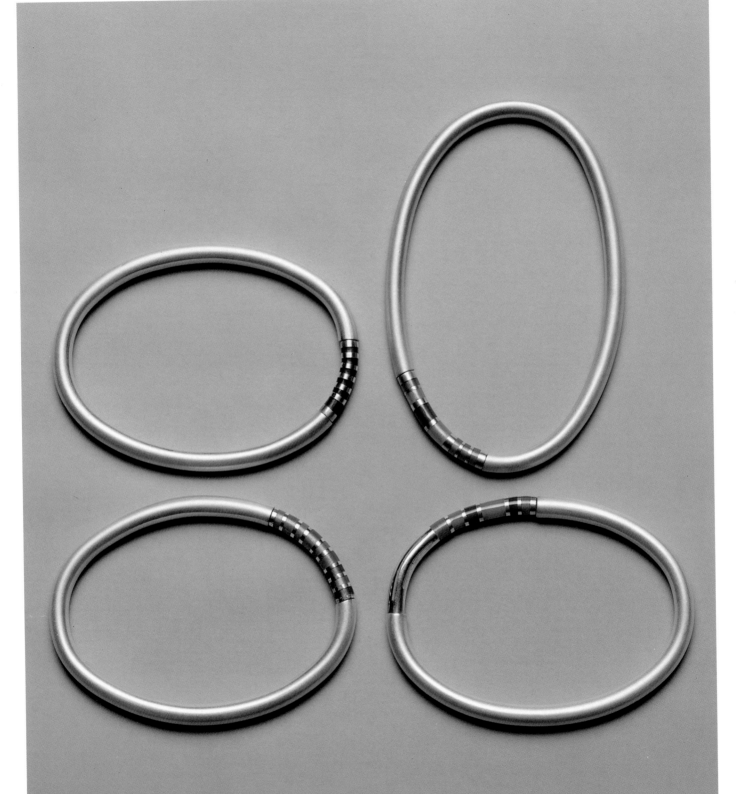

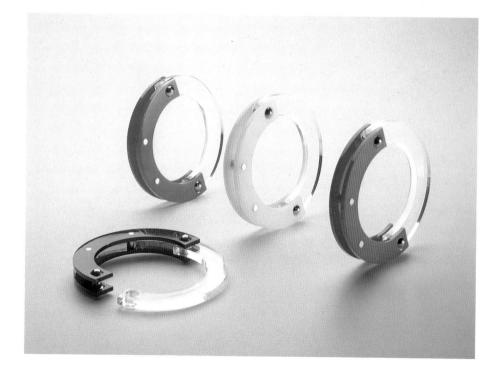

38 Four bracelets
   Helen Aitken-Kuhnen
   Silver (sandblasted), enamel
   7 cm
   Australia, 1983

39 Bangle, ring, both with
      interchangeable heads
   Paul Derrez
   Silver, perspex
   6 cm, 2 cm
   Holland, 1977

40 Bracelets
   Ben Wisman
   Acrylic with steel balls
   12 cm
   Holland, 1982

41 Brooches
Elisabeth Holder
Steel, silver
5 cm
UK, 1980

42 Rings
Giorgio Cechetto
Silver
2.5 cm
Italy, 1983

43 Rings
Wilhelm Mattar
Silver
2 cm
West Germany, 1982

44 Désir extraterrestre
Brooch, model for sculpture
Rita Grosse-Ruyken
Forged gold
22 × 9 cm
West Germany, 1982

45 Pendants
Johannes Kuhnen
Anodized aluminum, silver
8 cm
Australia, 1983

46 Brooches
Elisabeth Holder
Copper, gold, steel
7.5 cm, 4 cm
UK, 1980

47 Rings
Giampaolo Babetto
Silver, gold, resin
5 cm
Italy, 1983

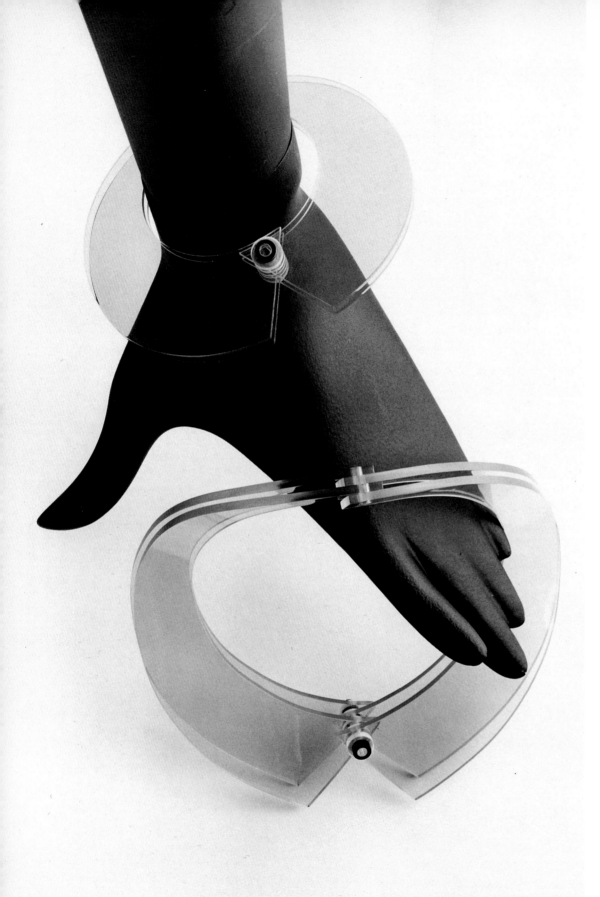

48 Bracelet, necklace
   Joelle Levie
   Plexiglass
   7 cm, 14 cm
   Belgium, 1983

49 Pins
   Joke Brakman
   Acrylic, steel
   7 cm
   Holland, 1982

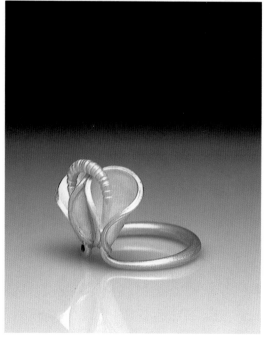

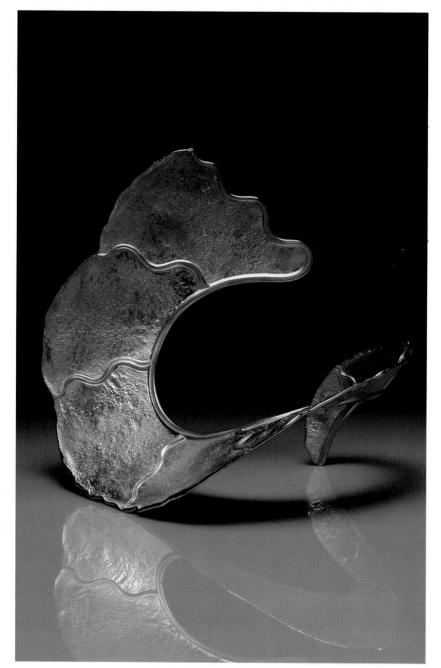

50 Ring
    Yehuda Tiglat
    Gold
    5 cm
    Israel, 1980

51 Bracelet
    Jackie Mina
    Gold
    8 cm
    UK, 1980

52 Necklace
E.R. Nele
Gold, silver, pearls
18 cm
West Germany, 1983

53 Necklaces
Rita Grosse-Ruyken
Forged gold
34–35 cm (pendants 5 cm)
West Germany, 1979

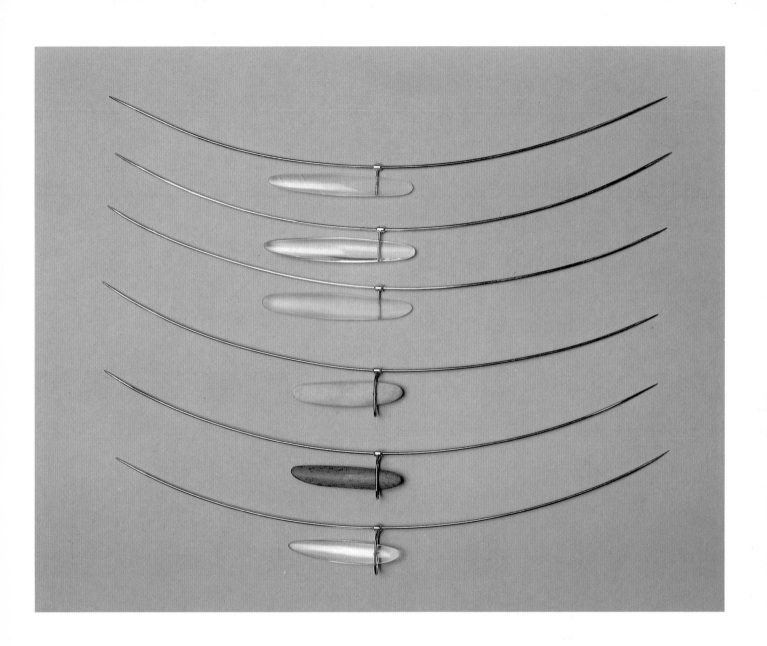

54 Necklace
   Suzan Rezac
   Silver, gold, nickel, copper
   18 cm
   USA, 1983

55 Pins
   Annie Holdsworth
   Gold, perspex, slate, brass, steel
   9 cm
   Australia, 1983

56 Push-through pins
   Johanna Hess-Dahm
   Anodized aluminum
   12 cm
   Switzerland, 1982

57 Z pin
   Brooch
   Gabriele Dziuba
   Painted wood
   15 cm
   West Germany, 1982

58 Cuboid
   Armpiece
   George Dobler
   Painted steel
   8 × 6 × 3 cm
   West Germany, 1982

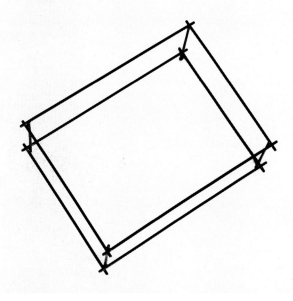

59 Neckpiece, body ornament
   Therese Hilbert
   Steel
   20–50 cm, flexible
   West Germany, 1983

60 Neckpiece
   Herman Hermsen
   Painted steel
   25 cm
   Holland, 1982

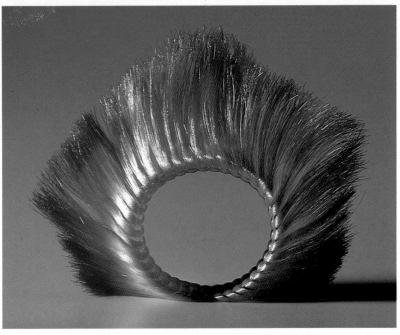

61 Wisp
    Armpiece
    Nora Fok
    Dyed nylon
    15 cm h
    Hong Kong, 1981,
        1982

62 Armpiece
    Nora Fok
    Dyed nylon
    14 cm h
    Hong Kong, 1981

63 Silver rib
    Bracelet
    Arline Fisch
    Knitted silver
    14 cm h
    USA, 1983

Overleaf

64 Brooches, rings, earrings
    Top left, then clockwise:
    Louise Slater, Paul Derrez,
    Cathy Harris, Louise Slater,
    Cathy Harris, Cathy Harris
    Acrylic, plastic coated
        paper, steel
    17 cm (largest)
    Derrez, Holland, 1981
    Harris/Slater, UK, 1983

65 Brooches, necklace
    Peter Niczewski
    Marquetry – natural,
        dyed wood veneers
        on plywood
    9 cm, 35 cm
    UK, 1982

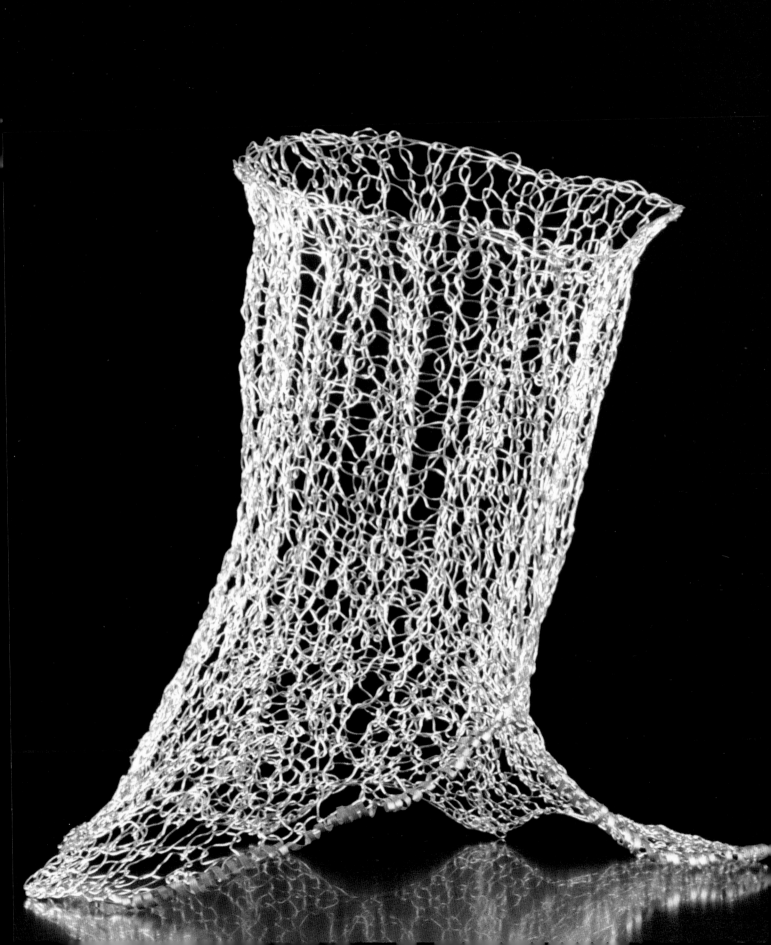

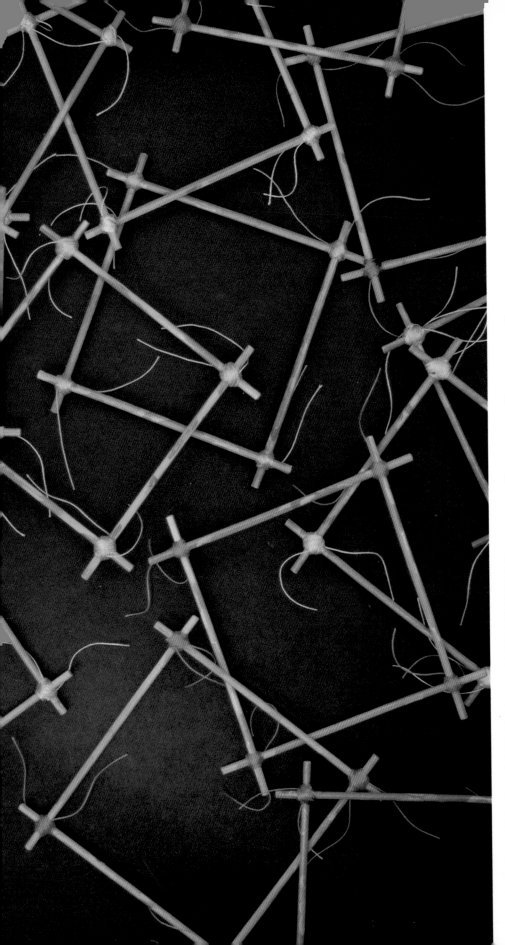

66 Bangles
   Ann Finlay
   Wood, silk thread
   8 × 8 cm
   UK, 1983, 1984

67 Rings
   Ann Finlay
   Acrylic, dyed aluminum
   2.2–2.5 cm
   UK, 1983

68 Brooches
   Therese Hilbert
   PVC, plastic, steel
   5–8 cm
   West Germany, 1982

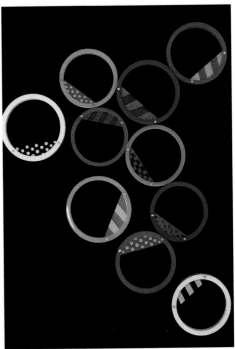

69 Neckpiece
   Therese Hilbert
   Steel, brass
   28 × 45 cm
   West Germany, 1983

70 Bracelet
   David LaPlantz
   Aluminum, ribbon wire
   8.5 cm
   USA, 1983

71 Brooch
   David LaPlantz
   Aluminum
   8.5 cm
   USA, 1983

72 Pins
   George Dobler
   Steel, epoxy-covered wire
   22 cm (longest)
   West Germany, 1983

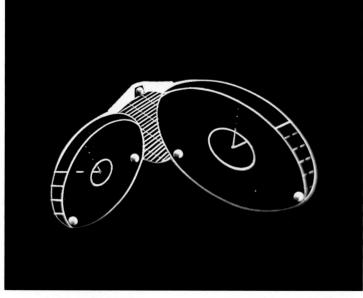

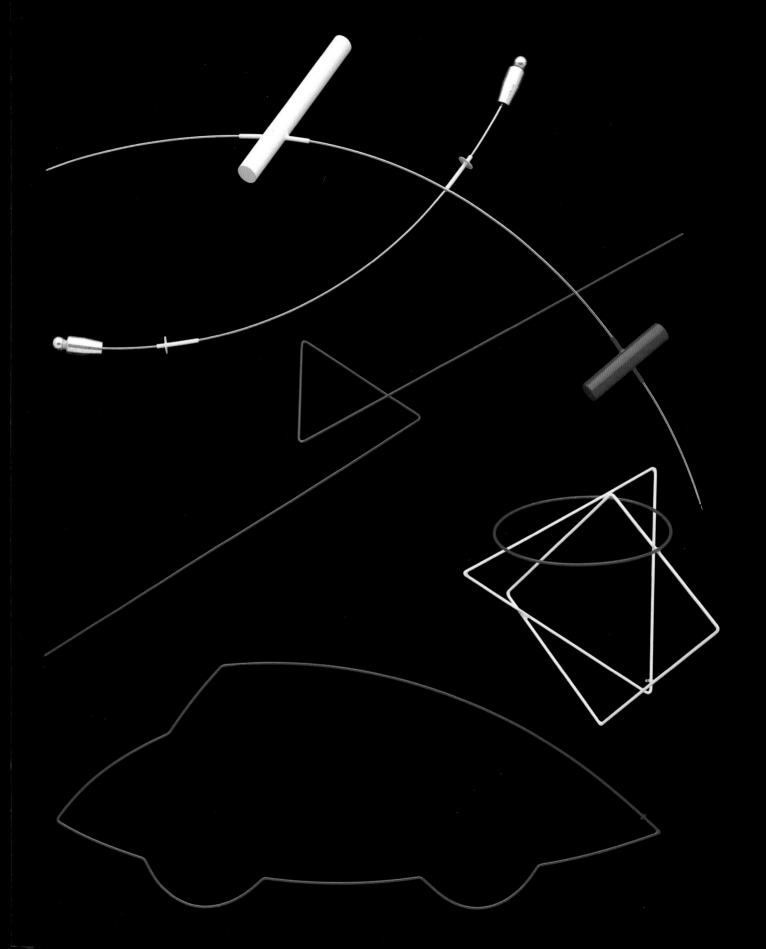

73 Brooch
    Edward de Large
    Titanium, silver
    5 cm h
    UK, 1976

74 Kite
    Brooch
    Joke van Ommen
    Anodized aluminum
    7 cm
    USA, 1983

75 Bangle, earrings
    David Tisdale
    Anodized aluminum
    4 cm, 9 cm
    USA, 1983

76 Three bracelets and pin
    Coen Mulder
    Anodized aluminum
    10 cm
    Holland, 1983

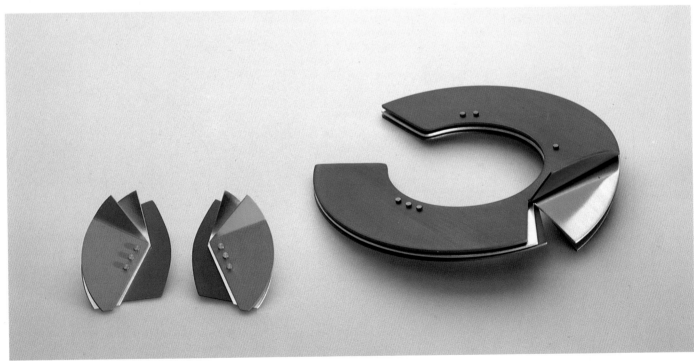

77, 79
Brooches
Johanna Hess-Dahm
Painted wood
15 cm
Switzerland, 1983

78 Two brooches
David Selkirk
Silver, copper, nickel
7 cm
Australia, 1983

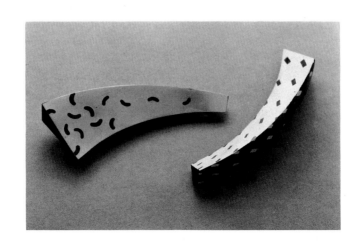

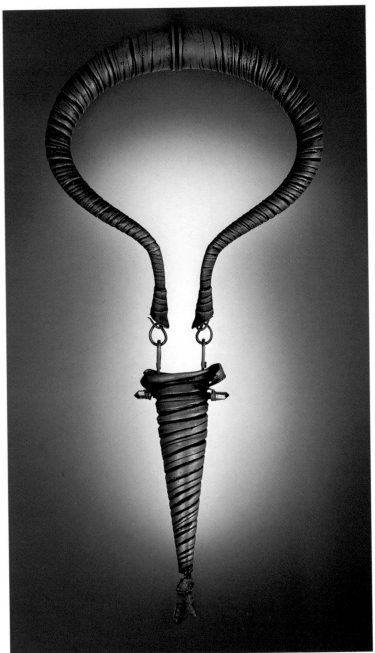

80 Neckpiece
Belinda Ross
Epoxy resin, acrylic
22 cm
UK, 1983

81 Torque no 68
Pendant
Stanley Lechtzin
Silver, silver gilt, amethyst
38 × 17 × 28 cm
USA, 1983

82 Bracelets
Cathy Wren (bottom)
Louise Slater (top)
Plastic, acrylic
10 cm
UK, 1983

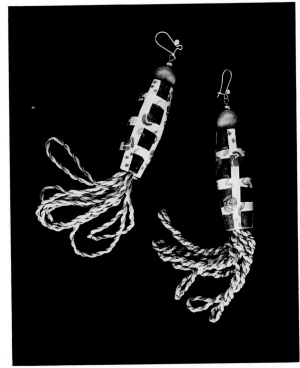

83 Necklace
 Louise Sant
 Brass mesh, silver,
  silver wire
 15 cm
 UK, 1981

84 Necklace
 Françoise Colpe
 Cotton, wool, feather,
  stainless steel
 25 cm
 Belgium, 1982

85 Looped cord earrings
 Annie Sherburne
 Silk, rayon, cord
 10 cm
 UK, 1982

86 Bracelet
 Lisa Gralnick
 Enamel on copper,
  ivory, feathers,
  metallic thread
 20 cm extended
 USA, 1982

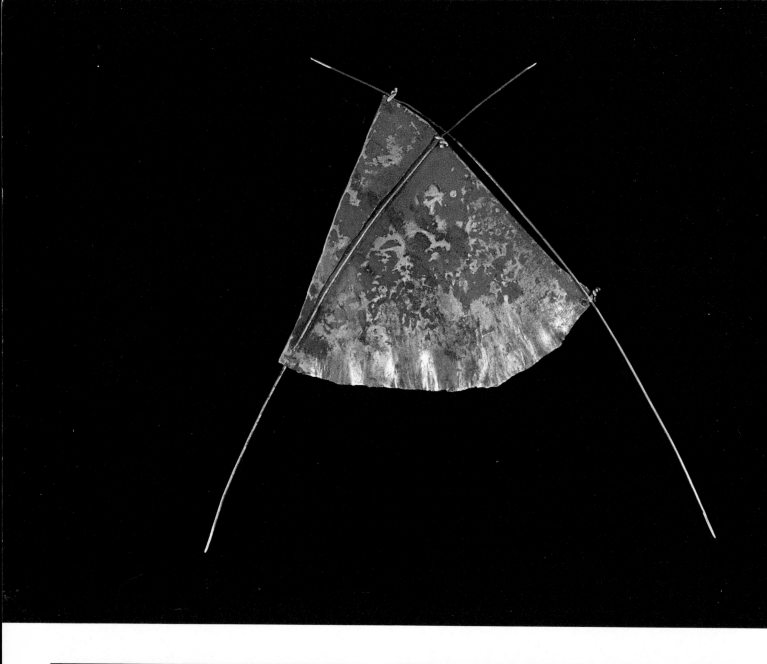

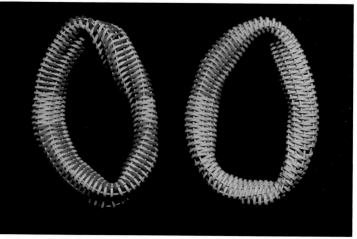

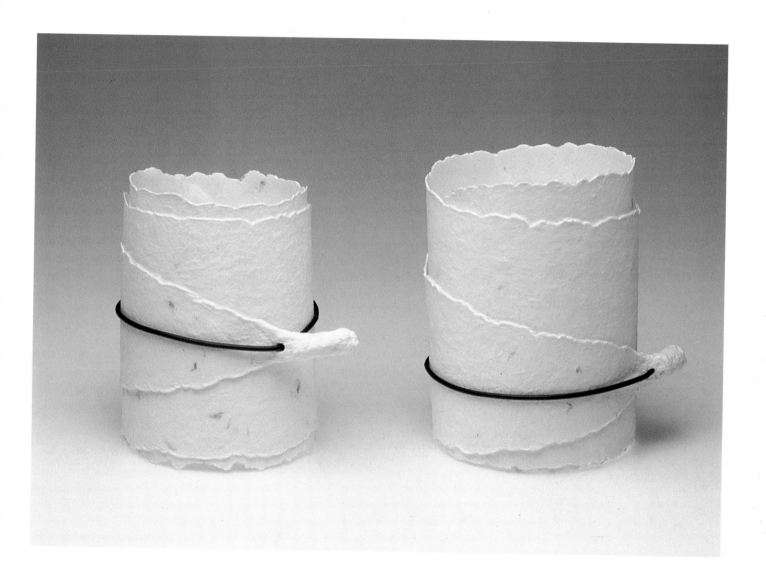

87 Brooch
   Marion Herbst
   Iron
   14 cm
   Holland, 1980

88 Necklace
   Mecky van den Brink
   Cotton
   25 cm
   Holland, 1983

89 Bracelets
   Beppe Kessler
   Rubber bands
   10 cm
   Holland, 1982

90 Armbands
   Willem Honing
   Papier-mâché
   11 cm h
   Holland, 1982

91 Prototype armpiece
Susanna Heron
Painted PVC
16 cm
UK, 1978

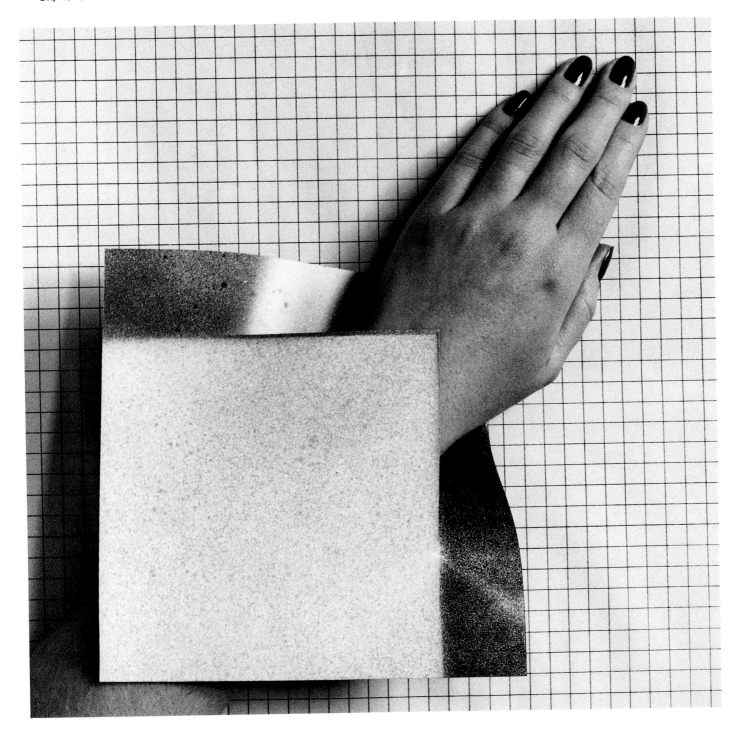

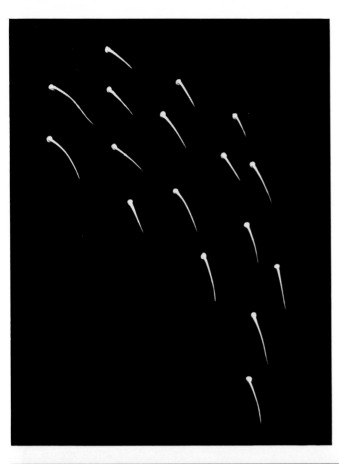

92 Pins
   Marlies Bächinger,
   Alban Hürlimann,
   Katharina Issler
   Rubber, brass pins
   2–3 cm
   Switzerland, 1982

93 Bracelets
   Emmy van Leersum
   Laminated PVC,
      coloured paper
   12 cm h
   Holland, 1982

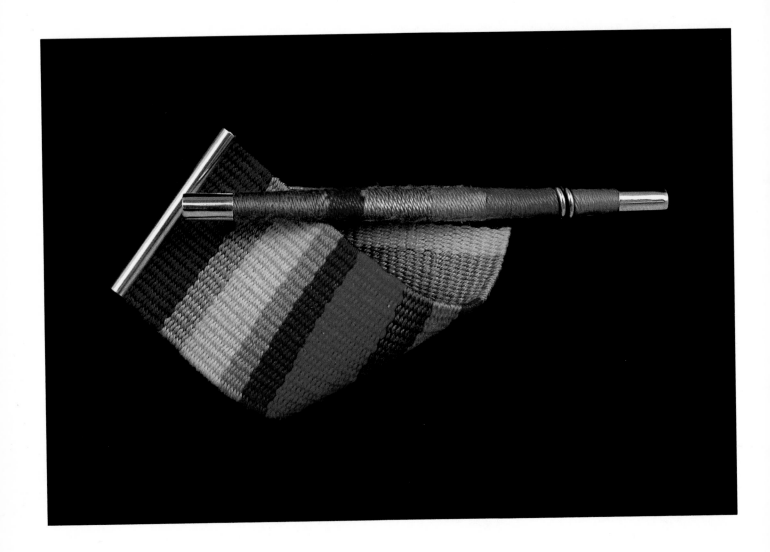

94 Brooch
   Marion Herbst
   Woven textile
   10 cm
   Holland, 1979

95 Necklaces
   Mecky van den Brink
   Knitted transparent nylon,
     dyed nylon
   15 cm
   Holland, 1982

96 Bracelets
    Maria Hees
    Leather
    10 cm
    Holland, 1983

97 Neckpiece
    Caroline Broadhead
    Wood hoop, dyed nylon
        tufts
    20.5 cm (hoop)
    UK, 1981

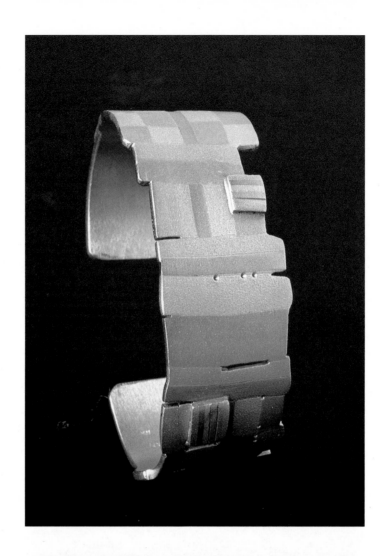

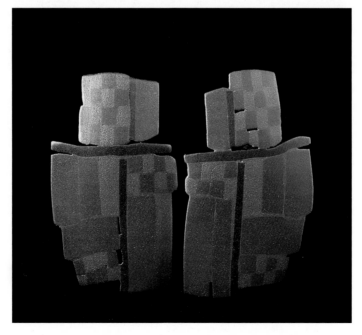

98, 99
    Bracelet, earrings
    Rena Koopman
    Coloured golds
        (sandblasted)
    7 cm, 5 cm
    USA, 1980, 1981

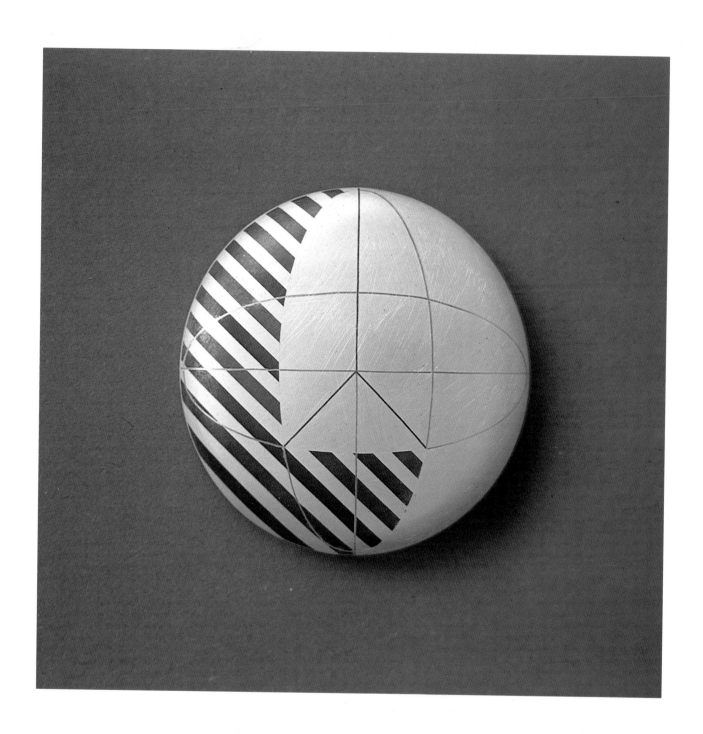

100 Brooch
Fritz Maierhofer
Silver, gold
6 cm d
Austria, 1977

101 Three armpieces
(left–right) Eric Spiller,
Caroline Broadhead,
Susanna Heron
Aluminum, wood, nylon,
  perspex
7–8 cm d
UK, c. 1980

102 Brooches
Charon Kranson
Steel, thread
5 cm, 8 cm, UK, 1983
Bracelet
Herman Hermsen
Steel
8 cm, Holland, 1982

103 Neckpiece
Barbara Alcock
Textile, steel
18 cm
UK, 1982, 1983

104 Bracelet
    Hans Georg Pesch
    Silver, titanium
    9.5 cm
    West Germany,
        1983

105 Bracelet
    Friedrich Becker
    White gold,
        emerald
    7 cm
    West Germany,
        1980

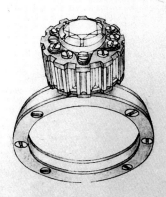

Joël degen
spring 1978

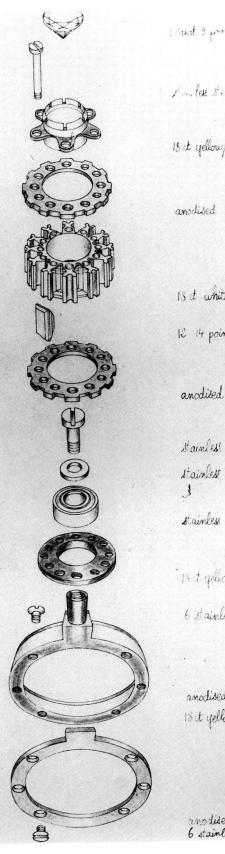

1 carat 3 points diamond

stainless steel screws . 16

18 ct yellow/white gold

anodised titanium

18 ct white gold

12 14 points diamonds

anodised titanium

stainless steel screw

stainless steel washer
3

stainless steel ball-bearing

18 ct yellow/white gold

6 stainless steel screws

anodised titanium
18 ct yellow/white gold

anodised titanium
6 stainless steel screws

'worry ring' consisting of a
revolving cylinder attached to
the shank by means of a
shielded ball bearing.
12 baguette diamonds are
arranged around the cylinder
and held in place by means
of titanium disks.
the ball-bearing is positioned
inside the cylinder between—
above — a tubular structure
into which is set a round
diamond — underneath — a
disk with 12 tapped holes which
receive the 12 screws which hold
the whole structure together.
the ball-bearing is secured to
the shank around a shaft with
a screw and washer.
the gold shank is faced on
either side with titanium disks
fastened to it by screws.

106 Ring drawings
    Joël Degen
    UK, 1978

107 Bangle
    Benny Bronstein
    Steel sheet, cable
    8 cm
    Israel, 1980

108 Bangle
    Joël Degen
    Anodized aluminum
    7 cm
    UK, 1982

109, 110
    Kinetic rings
    Friedrich Becker
    Steel
    3 cm
    West Germany, 1980

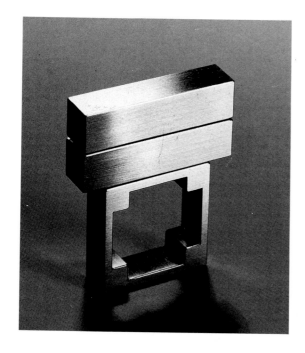

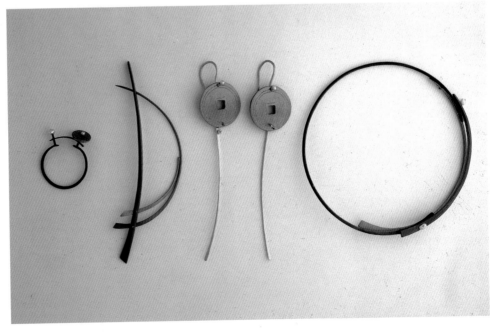

111 Bracelets
    Caroline Broadhead
    Nylon
    14 cm
    UK, 1981

112 Ring, brooch, earrings,
        bracelet
    Daphne Krinos
    Pearl, gold, anodized
        metals
    8 cm (largest)
    UK, c. 1983

113 Brooches, bangles
    Eric Spiller
    Anodized aluminum
    3–7 cm
    UK, 1980, 1981

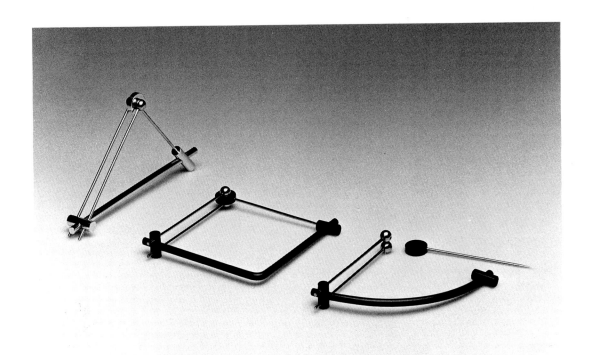

114 Brooches
Ben Wisman
Aluminum, steel
10 cm
Holland, 1982

115 ZigZag brooches
Carlier Makigawa
Brass, silver,
enamel paint
6.3 × 4 cm
Australia, 1983

116 Pins
Frank Bauer
Rubber, thread
2–4 cm
UK, 1982

117 Wing-Wave 3
    Combination
       neckpiece
    David Watkins
    Neoprene over
       steel/wood
    20 cm d
    UK, 1983

118 Mt Hagen Hoopla
    Neckpiece
    David Watkins
    Neoprene over
       steel/wood
    20 cm d
    UK, 1981

119 Necklace
    Jean-Paul Aleman
    Coiled wire covered
      in stitched silk
    30 cm
    France, 1982

120 Neckpiece
    Paul Derrez
    PVC, steel
    40 cm
    Holland, 1982

Overleaf
121 Neckpiece and
    two bracelets
    David Poston
    Titanium, forged
    14 cm, 6 cm
    UK, 1983

2

JEWELRY AS IMAGE

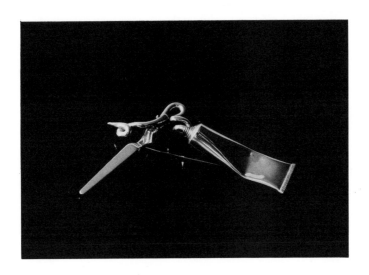

Mainstream
Figurative Work

Toothbrush and Paste. Brooch. John Plenderleith. Silver. 9.5 cm. UK, 1974

JEWELRY AS IMAGE
Mainstream Figurative Work

Translated into jewelry, bizarre fantasies may provide entertaining ornament. Of course, with abstract work, the observer and wearer can dance along with the maker through the choreography of form and harmony, but a direct appeal to the imagination is a necessary and attractive alternative. When confronted with something like Ralph Turner's international collection of plastic figurative jewelry, we have something to get to grips with immediately. Similarly, looking at Richard Mawdsley's brilliant but outrageous Gothic constructions, the viewer is immediately engaged in the question, 'What does it mean?'

Most of the objects in Fancy Goods (Ralph Turner's collection) are not especially bizarre or fantastic because they are only miniatures in plastic of humble day-to-day objects (such as breakfast cereal packets or hairdryers), with a leavening of images from the popular cinema (such as Tarzan). Nevertheless, many people are attracted by things in miniature – toy houses, model villages and, it appears, replicas of tins of baked beans as brooches. They all encourage good-humoured interest.

Laurie Taylor, an English sociologist, has written interestingly about Fancy Goods, although wisely he warns that writing about 'junk' jewelry can degenerate into 'junk' philosophy. He observed that the objects are a little downmarket of their wearer. And Taylor is right. Anyone with the slightest interest in the art and design world knows that etiquette about taste is as complicated as any other kind of social etiquette. You might, for example, genuinely like a concrete 'Cupid' ornament for your garden. If so, you risk being branded as tasteless, or downmarket, or *nouveau riche*. On the other hand, if everything else in your garden is well-thought-out and well designed, if your garden furniture is the design equivalent of the Mies van der Rohe *Barcelona* chair, you could have your concrete Cupid as a joke. Its presence would really let your friends know that you can distinguish good from bad, and more – that your tastes are so superior that having a little bad around the place simply cannot taint them. In fact, in some hands, with some people, the cleverness of the Fancy Goods style of jewelry could be stifling in its one-upmanship.

> Why do so many people love to wear such little jokes? [asks Taylor]. I think there are two main reasons. One . . . the desire to distance oneself from conventional jewelry which is redolent of security and a fixed life style; . . . The other, I believe, is the desire to call attention to oneself without striking too

pronounced a position. The little joke on the lapel or round the neck proclaims a mild sense of distance from conventional images but not a surrealistic subversion of everyday objects. It is something which tickles reality but leaves it undisturbed.

Tickling reality is a pleasant image but, if we are to believe Taylor, there is more to Fancy Goods than that. He commented: 'the miniaturised representations of commercial products are small insults to the real gods of our contemporary culture'. Not such a pretentious remark, perhaps. After all, it would be a brave young salesman who dared mock his company by wearing a comic version of it on his lapel.

Fancy Goods work is fun, it can be charming and its success is no surprise at all; Richard Mawdsley is quite different. Mawdsley's work is not coy, often it is not immediately attractive. Reactions tend first to be surprise, followed by praise for the skilled workmanship. The famous

131 Feast Bracelet impresses people because on the table there are intricately formed, well-turned miniature bottles, jugs, flagons, fruit and cutlery. Miniaturization is fascinating and in this case all the more so because the objects have a degree of verisimilitude which almost suggests that they have been used, that they are 'real' and not 'toys'.

However, as Janet Koplos, in her excellent *American Craft* article on Mawdsley brings out, he has doubts about the Feast Bracelet. He knows it is a technical masterpiece, but is it anything more? Is it aesthetically sound?

Mawdsley raises a difficult point for himself. Why should it be anything more than a virtuoso demonstration of his technical skills? What ambitions ought a jeweler to have for such a piece of work? After all, it is difficult (although not impossible) to imagine succeeding in making an aesthetic or spiritual *tour de force*, a *Last Supper*, say, to be worn on the wrist – it would be subverted by its built-in dinkiness in the same way that Hollywood biblical epics are subverted by the belief that verisimilitude is just a matter of getting all the details correct. The Feast Bracelet is really all right because it is a complicated, involved object without any specific allusions; it does not prompt the viewer into inappropriate inferences about 'meaning'. Koplos correctly points out that the bracelet is saved from dinkiness by the colour of the silver. Had it been coloured, naturalistically, it would have been unbearable: a Fancy Goods epic. As it is, if your taste favours such objects, then you will see it as a well-designed, extraordinarily well-made ornament.

One barrier to appreciating Mawdsley's work is not of his making. There is an abundance of figurative ornament on sale in department stores and gift shops: some is cast in metal, some in resin and some in porcelain. Most of this work is attempting to be 'lifelike' or 'detailed' and it is frequently nostalgic or backward-looking. Most of it is second rate. Arguably, however, it is precisely because there is so much of this 'junk' around that there is no danger of Mawdsley and other comparable figurative jewelers suffering from total critical disdain.

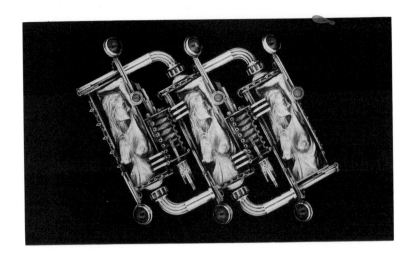

Goneril, Regan, Cordelia, Belt buckle.
Richard Mawdsley. Silver, lapis lazuli.
8 × 3 cm. USA, 1976–77

Some of Mawdsley's work is less literal than the Feast Bracelet. A piece such as the Medusa   156
pendant is 'interpretative' and works well enough as an image of the woman-beast whose hair is
composed of writhing snakes. Everything about the Medusa's torso echoes the horrible notion
of the snakes, not literally, but obliquely through its machine-like aspect. The piece appears to
be weak only at one point: the expression on the figure's face is not so much alarming as vaguely
fraught and middle-aged. Yet, this is a pendant for wearing and therefore not an occasion for the
completely grotesque. And it is arguable that such a caveat – in this instance, limiting the
grotesque – underlines once again one of the limitations of jewelry: each time it strays towards
sculpture the question, 'Dare anyone wear this?', is pressing.

The Goneril, Regan, Cordelia buckle is a particularly successful Mawdsley work; it is involved,
interesting and elaborate, a combination which works formally in terms of design and
composition, and intrigues imaginatively because of its imagery. We might puzzle about the
title. Why call it Goneril, Regan, Cordelia? If it is necessary to have literary allusions, why do the
three figures look like triplets? In *King Lear* the three women behave in different ways and look
physically different. In fact, it ought not to matter what literary labels are given to work of this
kind. Its potential for 'meaning' is not bound up with literature but in its more general appeal to
the modern Gothic imagination.

Occasionally, jewelry is used to make direct social or political comment – a point which is
developed further in respect of the Canadian David Didur, as well as Otto Künzli, in the next
chapter. Here we show several examples by the American jeweler, Ron Ho, including his
pendant Clockwork Cohn – a clear, rather simple, comment on the nature of modern,   158
industrialized work. The pendant illustrates what Gary Griffin referred to as the American
jeweler's concern with using his or her philosophy about life as the basis for jewelry (p.15). Ho's

piece asks the question whether it is desirable to spend one's time at the behest of machines in order to earn a living; at the end of one's working life, the price paid in time might be too great, the rewards too meagre. This particular work might thus be described as a minor *memento mori*.

Clockwork Cohn is not wholly typical of Ho's work which, as the illustrations show, tends to be concatenations of objects with no direct story. They are ornate assemblages. Ho has travelled extensively throughout the Far East – Japan, Indonesia, Thailand – as well as in India and Nepal. 'These travels exposed me to the ornate patterns of the oriental cultures which had a deep influence on my work and brought me back to my original heritage of being Chinese.' Ho's artefacts, the animals especially, are finely observed, sometimes stylized and grouped *en masse* to create a dense, ornate effect.

Another American jeweler producing figurative work is Bruce Metcalf, mentioned in the preceding chapter as an example of expressionism in new jewelry. Metcalf is one of the very few modern jeweler-sculptors whose work has sufficient substance to withstand translation from pin or pendant to table sculpture. His works also have wit – not that they provoke belly laughs, rather a kind or wryness; they are odd objects. Most of the pieces have several common ingredients, such as the sensation of movement and the implied notion that something is happening and that we have caught the action midway.

In the two pins called Unprotected Moon and Protected Moon the action is all bound up with defence and attack. By making the mechanical or manmade objects, such as the daggers, appear semi-organic and sentient, Metcalf makes the piece ambiguous but tongue-in-cheek. There are no specific meanings in Metcalf's work and 'sculptures' such as the 'Moons' pins are maddening if you are trying to crack open the visual metaphor; there is no point in trying. It is doubtful if even Metcalf himself can say convincingly what the works 'mean', because these are objects with their own life. What retains a viewer's interest is the fact that the work has just enough realistic content in it to catch the imagination. It is a quite different category of figurative work to Ron Ho's Clockwork Cohn, with its nailed-down meaning, or to the Betsy King nostalgic brooch.

The scale at which Metcalf's jewelry and sculpture works is important. Some of the table sculptures are fifty centimetres high, but the idea of making the same kind of images very much larger would be appalling. The peculiar objects Metcalf has created would look ridiculous if they were enlarged to metre-size or more. Part of the interest of all miniature work is that we peer into, and not up at, the maker's imagination.

One of the difficulties facing the figurative jeweller, as we noted in discussing the work of Richard Mawdsley, is the ever-present threat of 'dinkiness'. In one sense, making art in miniature is much easier than making it big because any flaws in composition, shape and form are not as noticeable as when they are scaled up. And what looks charming at the scale of a few centimetres is boring when enlarged — a fact that rather too many painters of stripy abstract canvases overlooked in the early 1970s. Yet there remains the 'trinket factor' — that sense of trivia which derives from the truth that at the very small scale there is no room for gesture or action. One of Metcalf's successes lies in the way in which he creates 'room' in his pieces.

Another jeweler who, like Metcalf, has avoided the trap of dinkiness is Manfred Bischoff. His work is attracting attention not least because he has come up with some new shapes and ideas for ornament. Bischoff has raided the heavyweight territories of fine art and come back with Greek pillars and an energetic bundle of linework from the Picasso-Matisse school of rapid drawing. By rights this 'plagiarism' ought to have meant failure, but these stolen goods have been made into something very much his own. By breaking the pillars, daubing them, making an assemblage of them, and by taking the Picasso-Matisse line and mangling it into a calligraphy of his own, Bischoff has produced new ornament. The wire portrait brooch, irrespective of its being a brooch, shows some adept modelling; it is a good piece of 'drawing'. The materials he uses, such as styrofoam and wire, are light and comfortable to wear, though wearability has not, it seems, played much part in the design of the work. It does not 'relate' to the body — very little figurative work does.

144–7

150

However, the Israeli jeweler, Esther Knobel, whose warriors and sportsmen have won an enthusiastic following in Europe, insists that all her pieces are intended to work on the wearer, that they are incomplete without the wearer. She has explained that she is interested in the

Object. Avner Axelrod. Plastic, cloth. 20 cm.
Israel, 1982

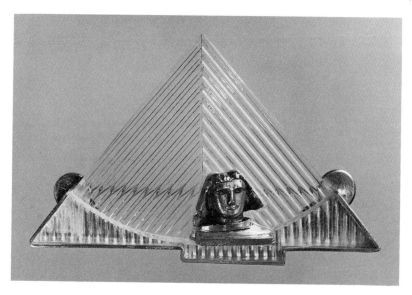

Brooch. Ulrike Bahrs. Gold, acrylic. 6 cm. West Germany, 1981

processes of jewelry-making, but makes no sketches or plans and has no idea at the outset how a finished piece will look. Tin cans are flattened into sheets out of which shapes are cut, and sometimes the pieces are embossed. The decoration of the warriors, with its reference to or association with camouflage, derives partly from some earlier work which for her was bound in with events relating to the wars between Israel and its neighbours. Realistically, however, Esther Knobel makes no claim that there is any 'political' content or metaphor for the wearer or observer of her work. For them the work is obviously decorative and playful.

Another Israeli, Avner Axelrod, has tried to make 'politics' into jewelry by producing 'medals'. Like Bruce Metcalf's work, that produced by Axelrod veers between wearable ornament and sculpture. Axelrod alludes to medals and uniforms through colour and the arrangement of shapes, but on second glance the dominant imagery is seen to consist of white mice, flowers and games redolent of childhood. Visually, these are interesting rather than pretty assemblages, but the 'meaning', their symbolism, is too esoteric.

Meaning and content in figurative jewelry usually breaks down into a straightforward division between the very literal, such as Ron Ho's Clockwork Cohn or Mawdsley's Feast Bracelet or Fancy Goods, and the open-ended ambiguities of Bruce Metcalf or Ulrike Bahrs, which let your imagination draw its own inferences. Figurative work goes adrift when the work is both ambiguous and yet intended to represent a narrow and specific range of ideas. Jewelers, like sculptors, sometimes have over-optimistic expectations that people will make the correct deductions about the specific meaning of their work.

The work of the Italian jeweler and sculptor, Bruno Martinazzi, might not seem to present any problems over interpretation and understanding, for it reproduces parts of the body. Yet these pieces are not, says Martinazzi, without meaning. The finger and hand pieces are intended to remind us of the 'hand as a creative instrument of knowledge and invention, and meant to establish a relationship with others'. And in his rings the concept of measurement is important because it is 'a means of understanding the universe of which man is a part'. It is important to note that Martinazzi's ambitions as sculptor have always taken on the large, humanitarian themes which may be too big for most jewelers to contemplate. Again, there is a question of scale, of needing space to construct a substantial coherent metaphor — a space not usually provided by jewelry. p.19 142–3

What all the best figurative jewelers are trying to avoid in their work, regardless of meaning, is cuteness. Cuteness bedevils jewelry in the same way that quick, slick, graphic tricks bedevil drawing. But in jewelry what can save a piece from banality is sheer quality of workmanship and the decorator's eye for good pattern — an excellent example from Britain is Sophie Chell's brooch. In some respects, however, the figurative jeweler puts his or her neck on the block more boldly than the abstractionist. With figurative work there are fewer opportunities for getting away with arbitrary decisions — there are too many ways in for the observer or wearer to pick up points and criticize. The lay critic can pick up on 'poor' modelling or composition in a way that is harder with abstract work simply because the 'ground rules' are less obvious. 125

Although it is unwise to prophesy, it none the less seems likely that the next few years will see more and more figurative work of innovation and interest, partly because the abstractionists are coming to a logical, albeit temporary, conclusion in their ideas about the forms jewelry can take.

Opposite
122 Pins
    Esther Knobel
    Painted tin
    15 cm
    Israel, 1983

123 Necklace
Esther Knobel
Painted tin
25 cm
Israel, 1982

124 Necklace
Esther Knobel
Painted tin
25 cm
Israel, 1982

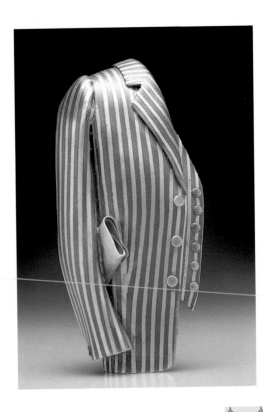

125 Pin
     Sophie Chell
     Anodized silver, gold
     6 cm
     UK, 1980

126–129
     Brooches
     From Ralph Turner's
       Fancy Goods Collection
     Plastics, resins, wood
     8 cm (largest)
     Australia, UK, USA, 1974–78

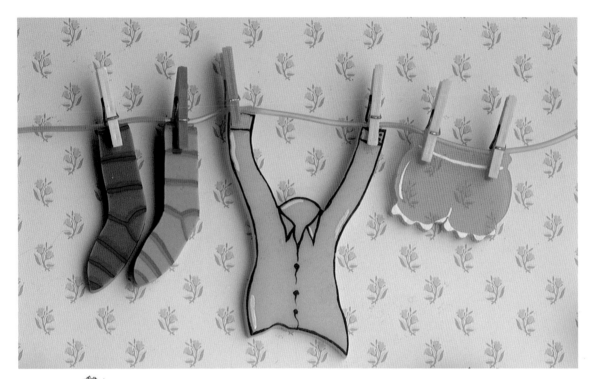

130 Pendants
   William Harper
   Gold, silver, enamel, pearl
   7 cm
   USA, 1980

131 Feast Bracelet
   Richard Mawdsley
   Silver, pearls, fabricated
   11.5 cm
   USA, 1974

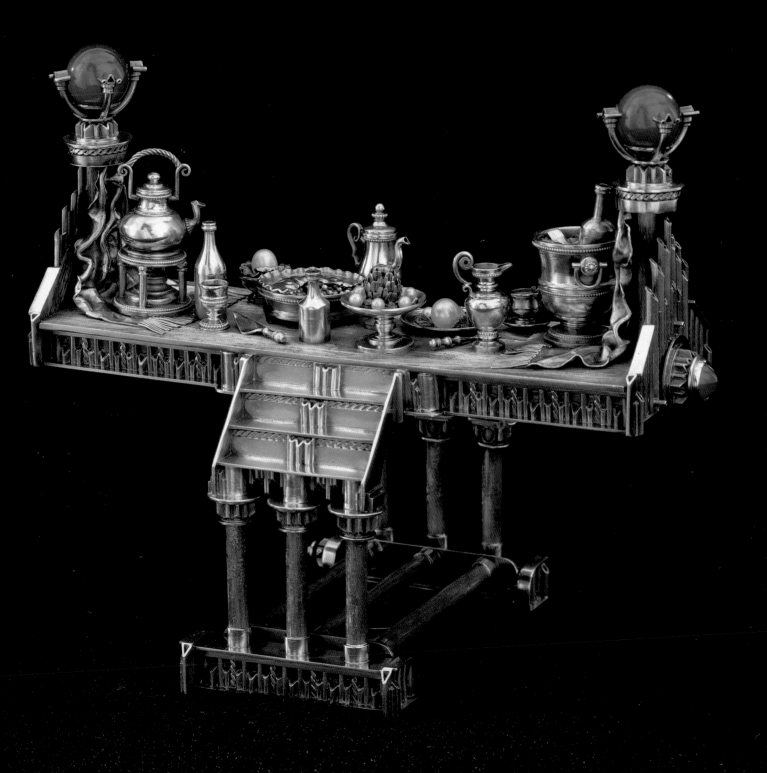

132 Rose
   Gijs Bakker
   Colour photograph
      in laminated plastic
   60 cm
   Holland, 1983

133 Chrysanthemum
   Gijs Bakker
   Chrysanthemum leaves
      in laminated plastic
   30 cm
   Holland, 1983

134 By The Sea
   Pin
   Betsy King
   Silver, shells, tin,
      plexiglass
   7.5 × 5 cm
   USA, 1977

135 Pin
   Esther Knobel
   Painted tin
   15 cm
   Israel, 1983

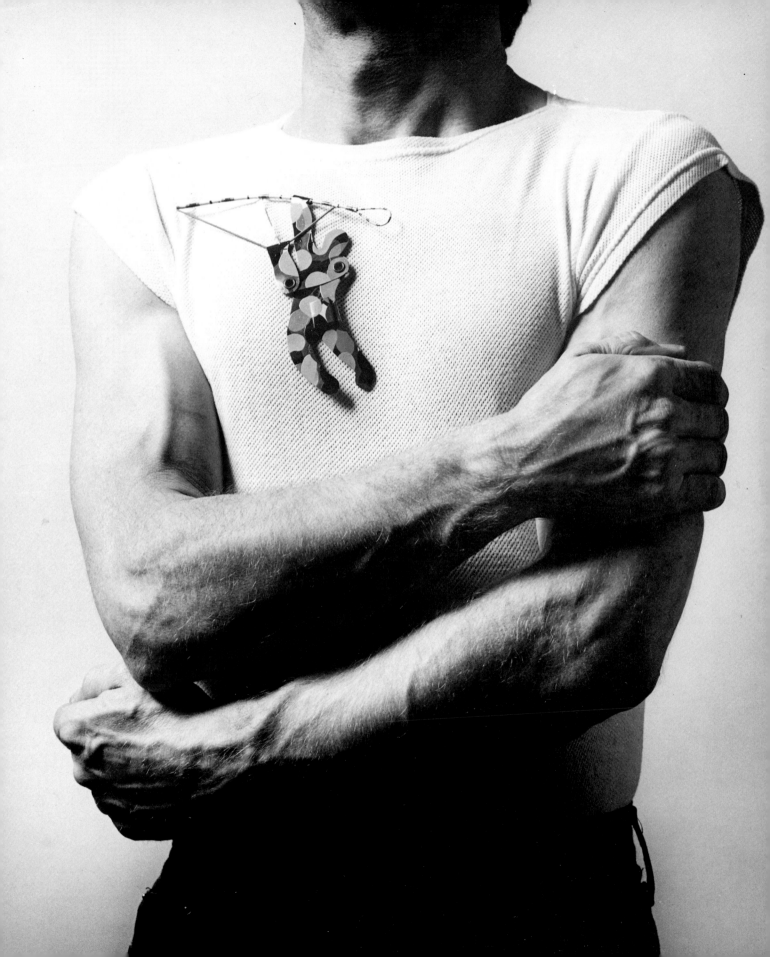

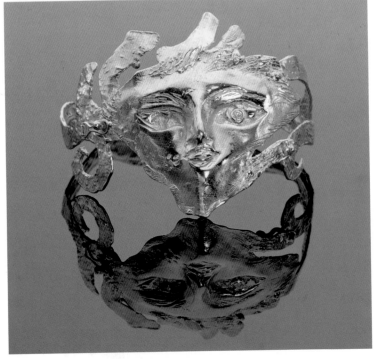

136 Treasures of the Orient
   Pendant
   Ron Ho
   Forged, fabricated
      silver, ivory,
      carved Chinese
      jade button
   22 × 9 cm
   USA, 1979

137 Bracelet
   E.R. Nele
   Gold, diamond
   7 cm
   West Germany, 1983

138 Gertrude's Bullish
      on America
   Necklace
   Ron Ho
   Fabricated silver with
      carved bullocks
      from India, beads,
      mother-of-pearl
   25 × 10 cm
   USA, 1981

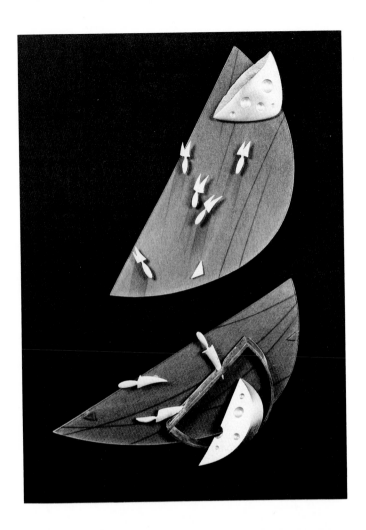

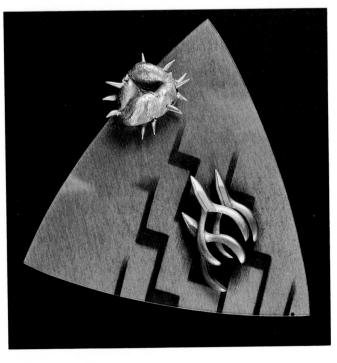

139 Unprotected moon
     Protected moon
     Pins
     Bruce Metcalf
     Silver, brass, acrylic
     11 cm h
     USA, 1981

140 Only Partly of This World
     Object
     Bruce Metcalf
     Silver, brass, acrylic, plastic
     20 × 12 × 3 cm
     USA, 1980

141 Pliers pursuing a prickly figure
     Brooch
     Bruce Metcalf
     Silver, brass, acrylic, plastic
     10 cm h
     USA, 1982

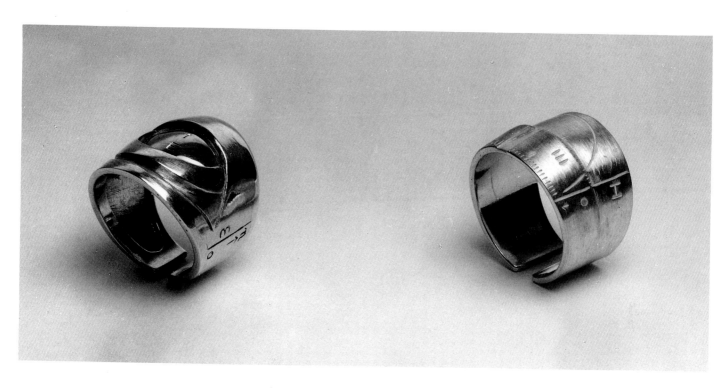

142 Energy
     Rings
     Bruno Martinazzi
     Gold
     2 cm
     Italy, 1980

143 Venus
     Brooch
     Bruno Martinazzi
     Gold
     6 cm
     Italy, 1980

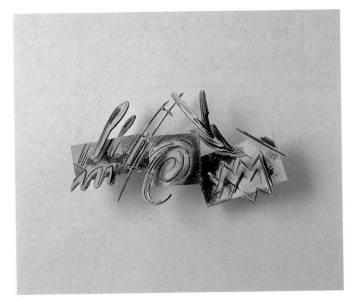

144–147
    Four pins
    Manfred Bischoff
    Styrofoam, wire
    15 cm
    West Germany, 1981–83

148 Brooch
    Gisela Seibert-Philippen
    Gold, ruby
    7 cm
    West Germany, 1977

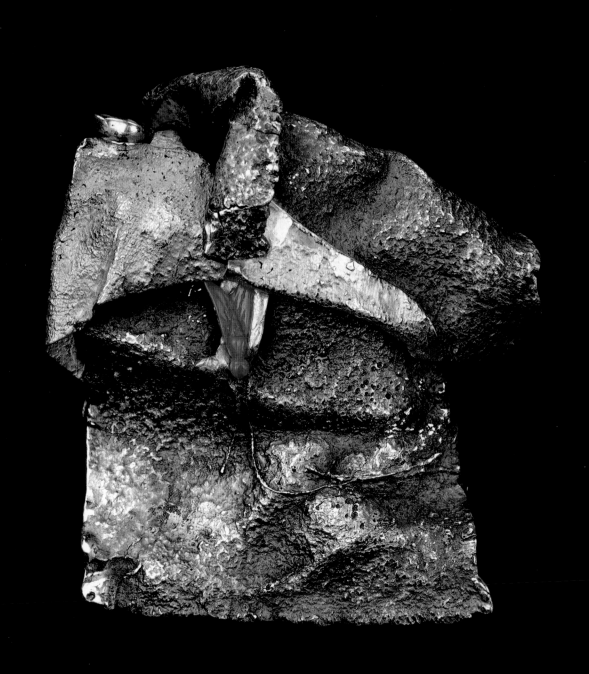

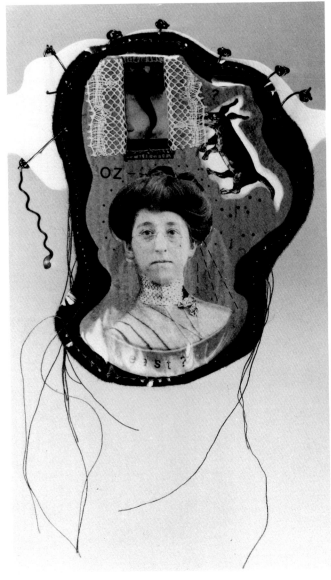

149 Brooch
   Ulrike Bahrs
   Gold, steel,
      screenprint on
      tinplate
   5 cm
   West Germany, 1980

150 Pin
   Manfred Bischoff
   Wire
   15 cm h
   West Germany, 1983

151 Oz East?
   Pin
   Julie Shaw
   Cardboard, felt,
      aluminum
   8 cm h
   USA, 1980

152 Bracelet, pin
   Ruudt Peters
   Acrylic, wire
   20 cm
   Holland, 1983

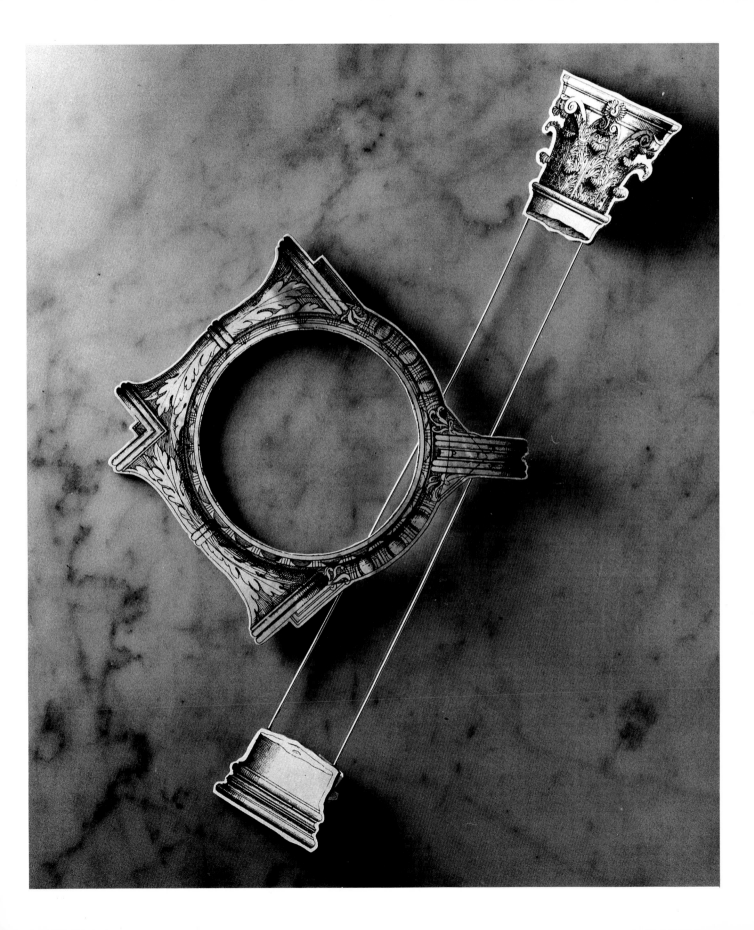

153 Brooch
   Hubertus von Skal
   Gold, steel, enamel
   5 cm
   West Germany, 1972

154 Into the Heart
   Pendant
   Ulrike Bahrs
   Gold, silver, acrylic
   6 cm d
   West Germany, 1979

155 Three rings
   Hubertus von Skal
   Gold, agates
   2 cm
   West Germany, 1972

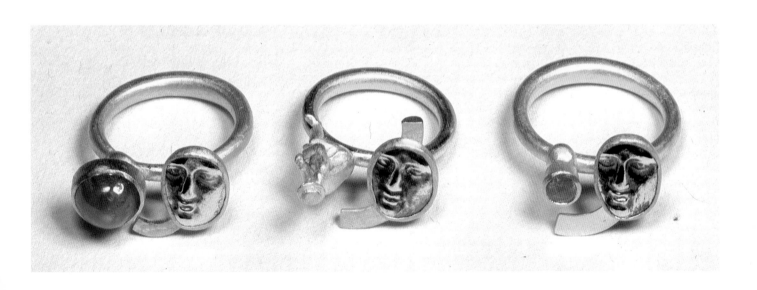

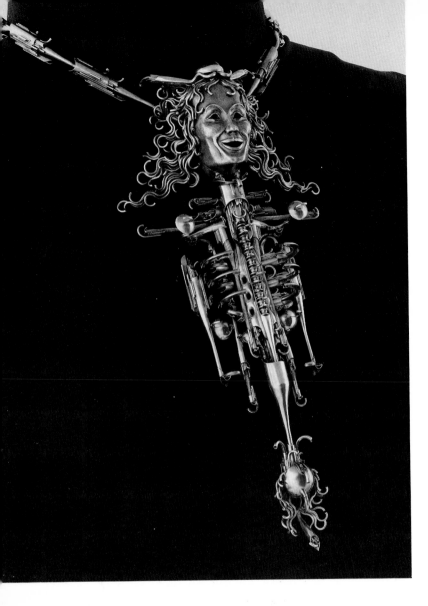

156 Medusa
   Pendant
   Richard Mawdsley
   Silver, lapis lazuli
   Fabricated, repoussé head
   20 cm l
   USA, 1982

157 Pendant
   Catherine Mannheim
   Silver, gold, ivory
   5 cm
   UK, c. 1978

158 Clockwork Cohn
Pendant
Ron Ho
Silver, bronze cast toy,
    eye glass lens, watch cogs
22.5 × 10 cm
USA, 1977

159 Pin
Glen Bodnar, Dan Donovan
Pencil, plastic paint brush,
    white metal, copper
15 cm l
USA, 1982

Overleaf
160 Brooches
Gary Wright
Silver
5 cm, 1.5 cm, 6 cm
UK, 1976

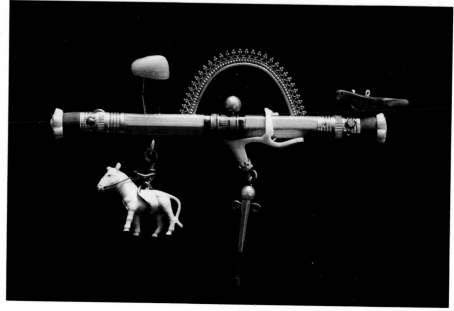

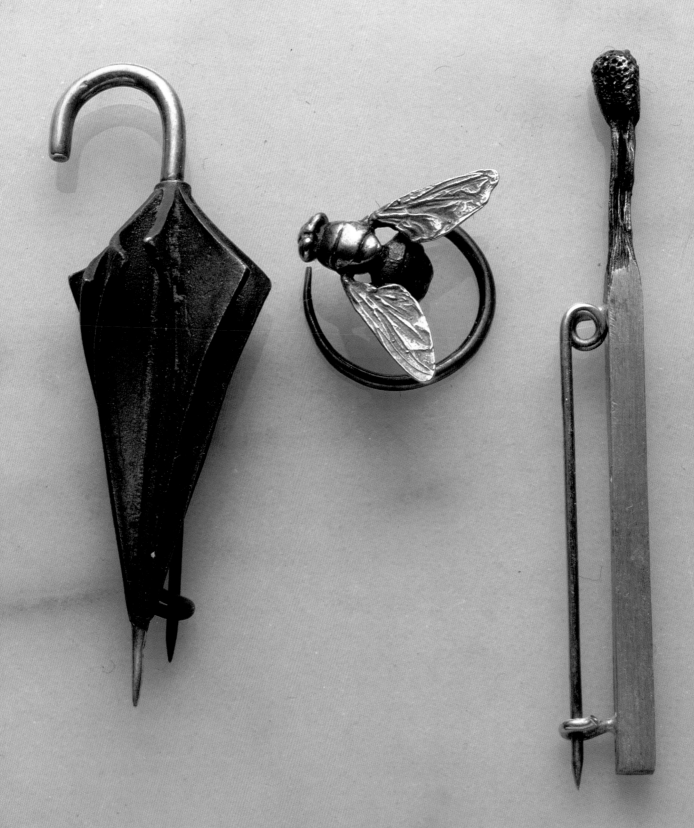

3

JEWELRY AS THEATRE

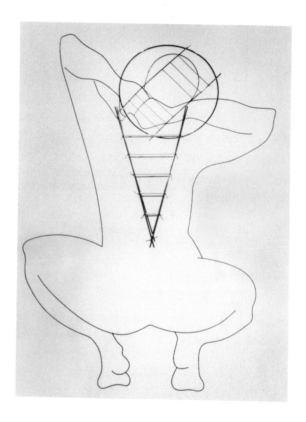

Radical Departures

Crouching figure. Ladder neckpiece. Julia Manheim. Wire, plastic tube. 1.6 m, 1.3 m. UK, 1983

JEWELRY AS THEATRE
Radical Departures

'It's unthinkable for a man to turn up at work wearing an earring . . .', says Horton. Horton, career diplomat, is a character in Paul Theroux's *The London Embassy*, which contains a long, witty passage dealing with the appropriateness (or not) of wearing jewelry. Horton is almost physically sick at the sight of his otherwise 'A1' communications officer wearing a single ring through his ear, but the man delegated to tell the officer that the earring has to be removed observes: 'I was surprised to find it a lovely earring. . . . It was the sort of detail that makes some paintings remarkable; it gave his face position and focus – an undeniable beauty. It was the size, and it had the charm, of Shakespeare's raffish earring in the painting in the National Portrait Gallery.' Nevertheless, the ring eventually goes, though it would spoil a good story to say how.

We all know that jewelry, like anything else a person chooses to wear, tells us about that person's taste and personality. But jewelry is rarely used by jewelers to make comment about the conventions and taboos surrounding either the making or the wearing of it. However, one man who has had a success in doing just that is the Swiss-born Otto Künzli, one of the most intelligent makers in the jewelry world and also one of the most sceptical.

The frequent play that Künzli makes with geometric shapes, with the block, cube and stick, has outraged jewelers and critics alike. They have responded by thinking that such activity is tomfoolery and childish, that anyone can do it; in any case, they ask, who would wear this work? Who indeed? The first point is that cube-and-block jewelry is not seriously intended as commercial ornament but as a reflection on jewelry and the limited conventions within which it works. Künzli makes us reflect on the narrowness, at any given point in history, of what society finds acceptable in dress. And the interest is not simply in reminding us that the conventions exist, but in highlighting the fact that they are arbitrary – that what is permissible changes.

Now it might be objected that this is all rather trivial. We know about fashion, but what Künzli demonstrates, or at any rate, what hostility to his work indicates, is how seriously people fight and argue when these otherwise 'arbitrary' conventions are broken. Künzli's subject matter deals in part with what we might term the 'Horton principle' – the unthinkable in body decoration. Some of Künzli's reflections, such as his Wall brooch, are taken to absurd extremes, 164 but other examples of his work are better mannered in their flouting of the rules. For example, if you re-read the Paul Theroux account of the man wearing the earring, and then apply it to the

Stick, cube, block pins. Otto Künzli. Wood grain wallpaper, hardfoam. Stick 35 × 2.5 × 0.5 cm. Cube 5 × 5 × 5 cm. Block 17 × 10 × 2.5 cm. West Germany, 1983

173 portrait shown in this chapter of the man wearing Künzli's House brooch, you will recognize an aptness in the description. The Künzli brooch might be said to give the face 'position' and to be the very detail that completes the portrait – and yet, by other criteria, it is absurd. The brooch is worn with a beautiful seriousness, and a dignity, which almost but not quite renders the object perfectly normal – it is the fine balance of the 'normal' with the 'unconventional' in this portrait that it gives it an edge.

There is a point about Künzli's work which needs clarifying. In producing his unconventional objects, he is not saying that they are, in fact, perfectly reasonable, obvious things to wear (although, in a different time or culture they *could* be). You do not demonstrate your great enlightenment and understanding of all things modern and liberal by rushing off in one of Künzli's creations. To do so is to miss the point. The point is to draw attention to the existence of conventions as real and binding, albeit at the same time temporary and arbitrary.

Künzli loathes the power and status that so much conventional jewelry parades through its use of precious materials. Consequently, he has devised a range of ornaments which is functional, pretty, cheap and, as far as possible, dissociated from money. These are the brooches

165–8 and pins he has produced in every conceivable geometric form, each with gaily decorated surfaces. Yet, even this work raises questions. If you look at the portraits of the two women – the one in a yellow sweater, the other a purple dress – it is probable that you will find their Künzli brooches perfectly acceptable ornament. You may or may not like the work, but these women, both of whom have the good fortune to be young and pretty, are perceived as being able to 'carry the work off'. But look then at the man wearing the (admittedly more elaborate) Künzli tie-pin. What is basically ornament, no different in kind to that worn by the women, appears radical and unconventional – a violation of the Horton principle. These pictures do more than draw attention to convention; they underline the reality of it by providing a demonstration which we can see for ourselves of what is acceptable and unacceptable in everyday life.

With work of this kind, adjectives such as 'witty' and 'humorous' are often scattered around with abandon but without much evidence. As an example of Künzli's wit, we offer the man 168 wearing the floral, decorated brick. This brick upstages a number of male-dominated conventions, from the vaguely lecherous (or, alternatively, very formal) flower in the buttonhole, to the politician's rosette. It is an example of well-mannered rudeness. In *A Map of the World*, a play by the British writer David Hare, a young man gets very annoyed with a middle-aged man, who has been polite but rude to him. Then he explodes: 'You're like all those people who think that if you say "Excuse me" at one end of a sentence and "Thank you" at the other, you are entitled to be as rude as you like in between.' In between the politeness of his object and that of his models, Künzli is being quite rude.

Künzli's work, like most of that shown in this section, is at its most effective in photographs where the maker has complete control over all aspects and the wearer and the object are fixed into a single, photograph-jewelry event. The extent to which the photograph and art gallery dominate radical work can be seen simply by looking through the pictures here. This is also true of Marjorie Schick's huge neckpieces, which are clearly unwearable in the day-to-day sense of the term. Her large works are ritualistic, ceremonial, with more than a nod in the direction of tribal dress and tribal dance.

There is a tendency among critics to debunk the sort of work produced by Schick as being flash-in-the-pan – a quickly worked-out idea with no particular development behind it – but that is not the case. Schick, who trained first as a metalsmith, began in 1967 to make large papier-mâché bracelets. Papier-mâché enabled her to work large whilst keeping the weight under control, and it also provided her with a surface to paint. Later she abstracted both line and colour from these works and gradually evolved her current compositions.

Schick has pushed the components of twentieth-century abstract art to its proper decorative 198 conclusion. Yet, whilst this makes her work a decorative art, it does not make it jewelry; it has become an abstract art with its roots in jewelry. This obvious, but important, distinction saves us from a world of nonsense. At the moment, some 'artist'-jewelers are unnecessarily confusing themselves – and others – by insisting that their work is jewelry despite the fact that it cannot be worn except, possibly, under very limited circumstances.

Left, Armpiece. Marjorie Schick. Papier-mâché. 12 × 18 cm. USA, 1969

Above, Pins. James Evans. Lint, cotton. Canada, 1983

185, 196   Pierre Degen is the most controversial 'craftsman' to have shown under the auspices of craft or decorative art in either London or New York. His recent work has consisted of performance-based pieces or 'sculptural' works and has involved all manner of large objects, including large ladders and huge black balloons on sticks. It is possible that certain critics understand, or at least articulate, Degen's ideas more clearly than Degen himself. Certainly there was a sigh of relief, mixed with enlightenment, when *Crafts* magazine published its review of Degen's London exhibition (September 1982). The review was written by one of Britain's younger and most important poets, Christopher Reid. In order to appreciate Reid's analysis fully – and perhaps to note also a degree of poetic sympathy – it is useful to know that he is one of the 'Martian' poets – a school of influential British writers taking their name from a poem entitled 'A Martian Sends a Postcard Home' (by Craig Raine). This is a poem in which the familiar world is seen through the eyes of an alien. And so, to quote from Reid:

> Degen has told me how he delights in the appearance of ordinary objects – brooms, garden implements, a window-cleaner's apparatus – but not so much for the way they have been made, as for the spectacle they provide in their workaday context. A number of things he likes are being shown in his exhibition, alongside pieces made by him. The point is that one is enabled to see these otherwise normally neglected artefacts with greater vividness in the ironic light that Degen's work casts upon them. I can say from my own experience that, after watching their maker trying on this piece and that in the setting of his studio, it was possible to step into the outside world and feel a surge of innocent

Large loop. Pierre Degen. Fiberglass, string.
160 cm d. UK, 1982

amazement at the great radiant sail-like contraption that we have learned to call an umbrella . . . or any of the other mysterious properties with which the inhabitants of our civilisation have chosen to extend or encumber themselves.

Undoubtedly such an interpretation is reasonable; it is also coherent. Degen's work has taken upon itself the wider category of speculation and interpretation associated with the fine arts, with sculpture in particular. And it is interesting that to do this Degen has had to work on the large scale; it confirms the view expressed earlier that one of the limits which keeps jewelry to an essentially decorative function is its literal lack of physical space in which to create gesture and to develop metaphor. Degen has had to sacrifice practical wearability (an essential characteristic of jewelry's definition) in order to make, comment and explore ideas about the sorts of things we wear or carry. The work once had some roots in jewelry, but recently has had to be taken outside jewelry in order to comment and reflect upon it.

Less controversial is Susanna Heron, whose development Ralph Turner has explained in his historical review. She was one of Britain's most important modern jewelers, although now she is developing as a sculptor. Her work, which has explored geometry and colour in wearable ornament, progressed to 'wearables' with a kinship to clothing but, by 1983, it was clearly to be looked at and not worn. If it was ornament at all, it was ornament for a room. Nevertheless, her wearables have given us some beautiful examples of decorative art, not least the blue and red 171–2 'hat' illustrated here.

161 Susanna Heron and, most importantly, Caroline Broadhead have been dominant among the radical jewelers in Britain, but Broadhead's recent radical (as opposed to her mainstream) offerings have tended towards clothing. Her 'veil' or 'headpiece', which we illustrate, is clearly an extreme work in the sense that it is seen at its best, and can be worn only at its best, on a model in a gallery or posing for a photograph. Nevertheless, the same piece, because of its flexibility, can be worn more practically by collapsing it into different, more convenient shapes, as a 'ruff' around the neck or pulled down across the shoulders.

What marks the different futures for the two makers is the likelihood that Caroline Broadhead's work will remain wearable. Susanna Heron, on the other hand, became interested in the grouping of objects and the scope that these groupings then provide for sculptural metaphor. These objects may, or may not, continue to take with them the references to the body.

Whatever the precise 'content' of work by people such as Heron or Degen, it is generally oblique and metaphorical. As we have seen, very few jewelers attempt direct socio-political comment in their work. This is not surprising. Apart from the fact that very few makers see jewelry as an appropriate medium for such comment, it is also the case that many of them, with Otto Künzli a notable exception, are rather insular. Ideas and issues beyond the world of the decorative arts do not inspire their work. It can thus come as a considerable surprise when an overt political comment is attempted in the context of a jewelry exhibition. David Didur, the

162 Canadian jeweler, produced a 'necklace' and pendant called Medal for Dishonour for the exhibition *Jewelry In Transition*. The work was made of live and dead matchsticks, firecrackers and thread, and the pendant was in the shape of the United States of America. Didur listed his materials more radically: Political Firecrackers, Industrial Iron (pendant), Strike Anywhere

Cigarette Performance Pack. Tom Saddington. Steel. 180 cm. UK, 1980

Matches, Short Fuse, and Threads of Credibility. Here was an anti-cruise missile protest, conceived on the premise that you never know when it (or a cruise missile) is likely to blow up. It was shrewd of Didur to make the piece for an exhibition likely to attract publicity but, of course, its success was dependent upon its rarity; if every jeweler started making protest jewelry then its impact would disappear, unless it was widely worn.

The political imagination is also at work in the recent examples produced by West-German jeweler Wilhelm Mattar. Mattar's work is a mixture of the abstract and the figurative, but it has about it a hint of brutality which is surprising and mildly discomforting in jewelry. The 'earpieces' 192–5 are placed in the arms of toy soldiers to become banners or weapons, and, as the portrait photographs show, when worn they can be given a degree of menace. Here we see jewelry played up as a symbol of machismo, while usually it is purely ornamental. With the implied violence, there are also, perhaps, sexual connotations, although it is too easy with this sort of work to begin manufacturing metaphors and associations – like pulling an endless string of flags from the conjurer's hat. Mattar's work presents an upmarket, radical chic version of Punk, which has taken various forms since it began as a late-1970s fashion among adolescents who wore razor blades, nails and safety pins to establish a version of tribal identity for themselves and to distance themselves from adult authority.

Graham Hughes, editor of the London magazine *Arts Review*, was quite right when he said that the most effective parallel between radical jewelry and other art forms was the theatre. Hughes, however, intended the parallel to be a criticism. He said (*American Craft*, September 1983): 'On stage, the audience can enjoy the fun and beauty and fantasy and visual philosophy of all sorts of strange gear but can't appreciate them with the full senses, for the simple reason that the footlights are in between. Stage props don't look too good in real life because you get too close to them, and you start analyzing them with those senses which the theater designer puts out of reach: touch, weight, texture, even smell.' He concluded that such work is really a statement for the stage, not real life. This criticism would be sound had the makers he was criticizing (Degen, Heron, Broadhead and others) maintained that their radical work was simply wearable ornament. In fact, most of the work pictured in this section is exploring ideas, much as the theatre is used for exploring ideas. As such it offers, as the theatre offers, a number of possibilities for criticism, debate, acceptance or rejection, with the knowledge that, in the end, the audience, the purchaser and the wearer always decide.

Opposite
161 Neckpiece, veil
   Caroline Broadhead
   Nylon monofilament
   45 cm, 25 cm d
   UK, 1983

162 Medal for Dishonour
Neckpiece
David Didur
Firecrackers, iron, matches, cotton
27 × 21 cm
Canada, 1983

163 Necklace
Stirling Clark
Pasta
37 cm
UK, 1983

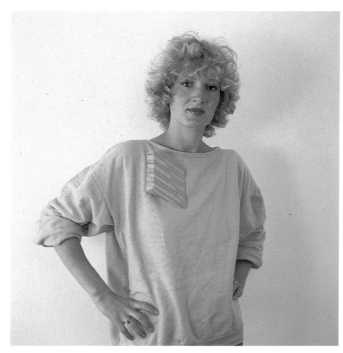

164–168
Brooches
Otto Künzli
Wallpaper, hardfoam
Top left, 43 × 20 × 5 cm

Top right, 13.5 × 12 × 5 cm
Bottom left, 23 × 11 × 2 cm
Bottom right, 19 × 14 × 1.5 cm
Opposite, 13 × 9 × 6 cm
West Germany, 1983

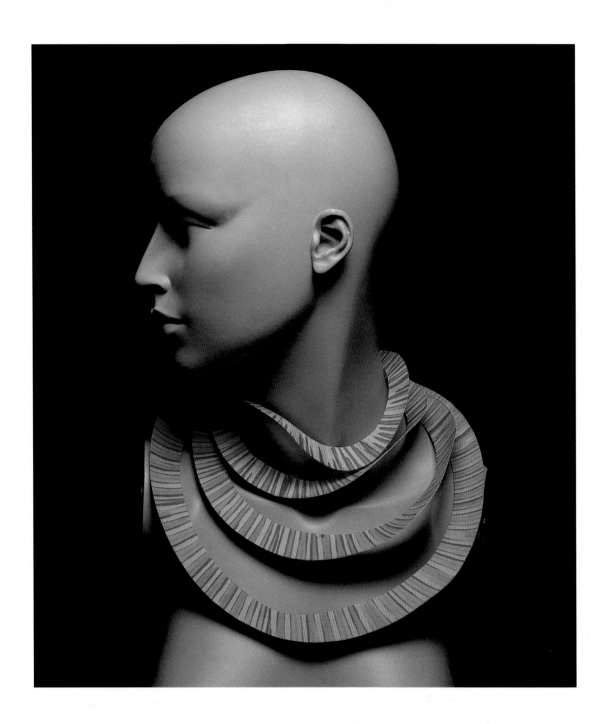

169 Ladder neckpiece
    Julia Manheim
    Plastic tube
    120 cm
    UK, 1983

170 Paper neckpiece
    David Watkins
    Paper spiral
    20 cm
    UK, 1983

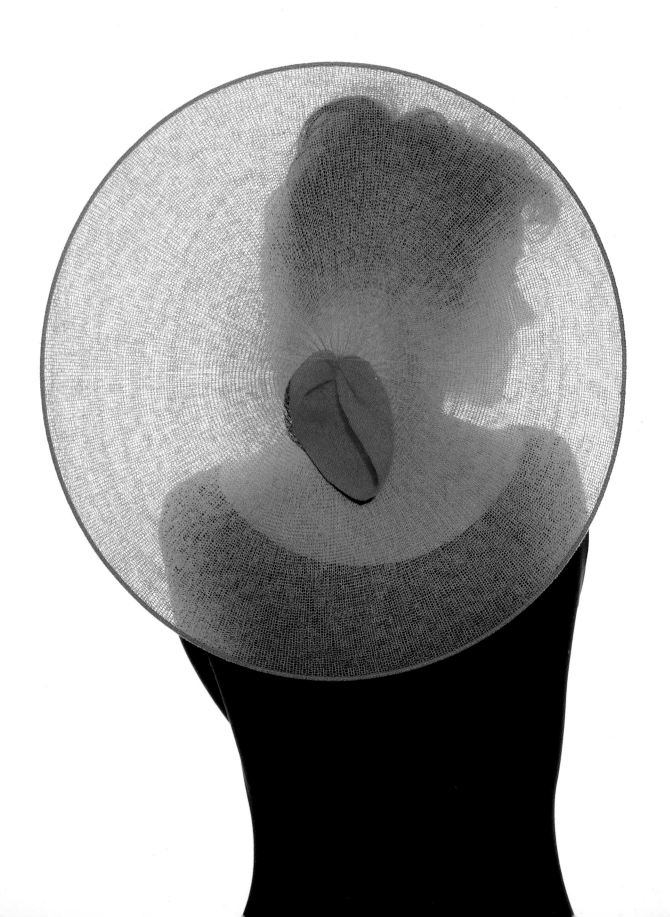

171 Wearable
   Susanna Heron
   Cotton on wire frame
   46 cm d
   UK, 1982

172 Wearable and non-wearable objects
   Susanna Heron
   Painted papier-mâché, cotton, nylon,
      wire
   Largest wallpiece, 60 × 10 cm
   Largest wearable, 62 × 22 cm
   UK, 1981–82

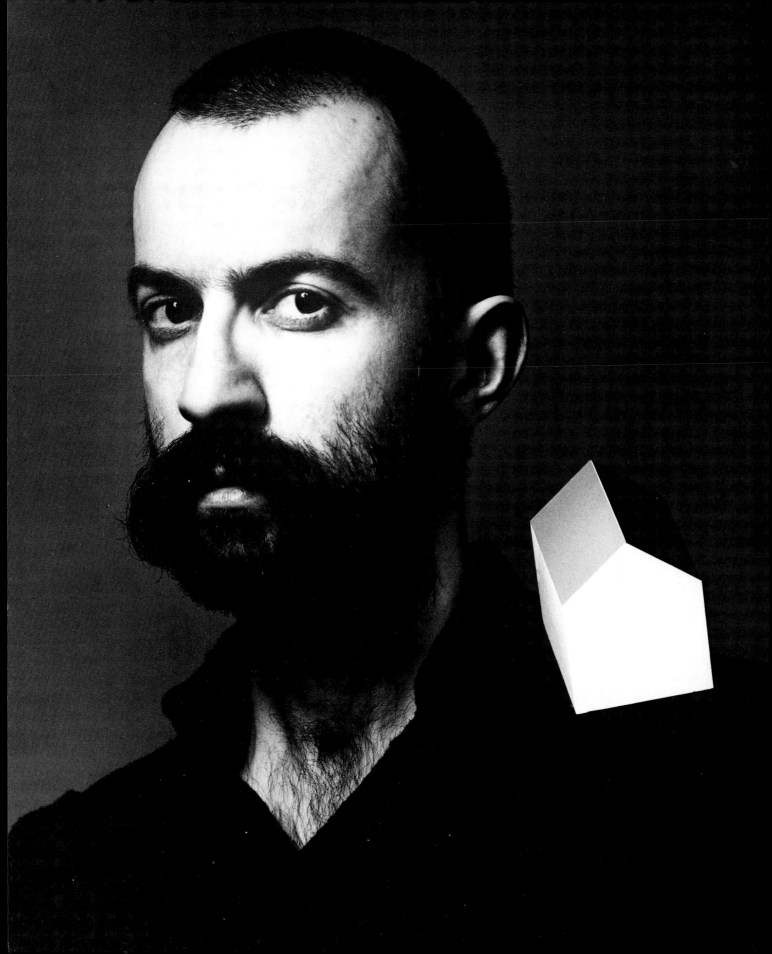

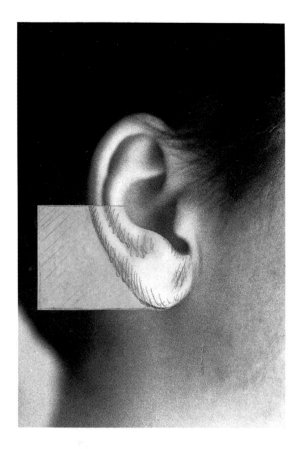

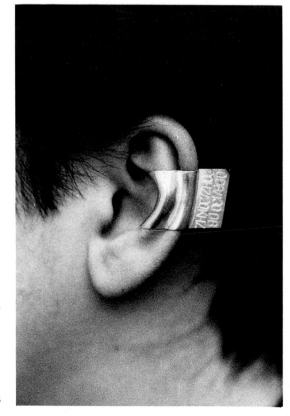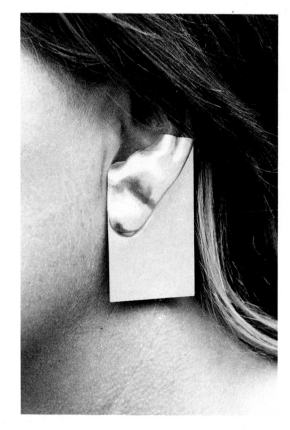

173 House
   Brooch
   Otto Künzli
   Paper, hardfoam
   8 × 6 × 7 cm
   West Germany, 1983

174–177
   Earpieces
   Gerd Rothmann
   Silver
   2.5 cm
   West Germany, 1983

178 Shoulder and body piece   179 Head-, neckpieces
Lam de Wolf   Michael Petry
Shredded fabric   Paper and paint
120 cm   28 cm
Holland   USA, 1983

180 These Shoes Are
        Made for Walking
    Performance-based
        jewelry
    Michael Petry
    Paint, paper
    6–15 cm
    USA, UK, 1983

181 Shirt with
        seven sleeves
    Caroline Broadhead
    Silk
    2.5 m
    UK, 1983

182 Shirt with
        seven necks
    Caroline Broadhead
    Cotton
    2.5 m
    UK, 1983

183 Neckpiece
    Susan Sanders
    Knitted latex rubber,
        fabric, shells, beads
    35 cm
    USA, 1982

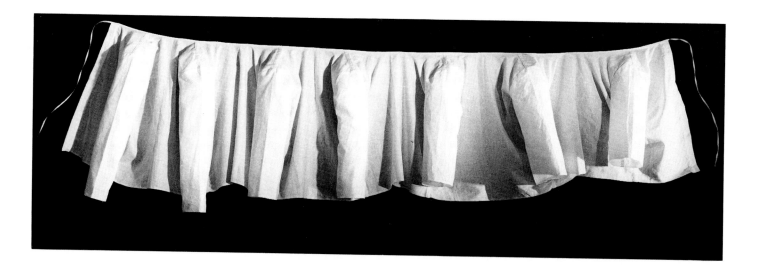

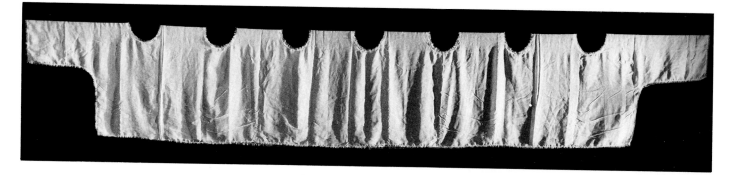

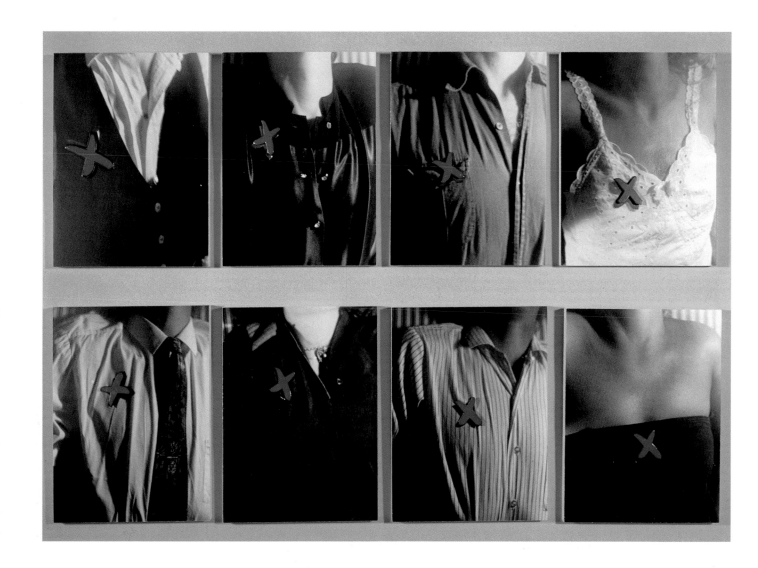

184 Party Jewelry
   Richard Karpyshin
   Eight framed life-size
      photographs, red
      enamelled crosses
   8 cm
   Canada, 1983

185 Personal environment
   Pierre Degen
   Wood, string
   140 × 140 cm square
   UK, 1982

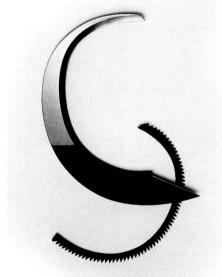

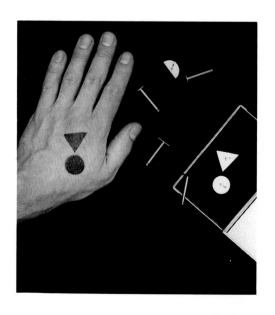

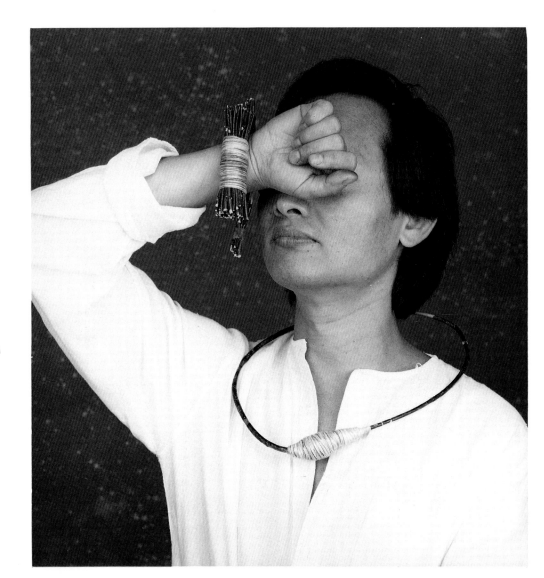

186 Ready Made
   Catalogue cover
   Exhibition at
      Galerie Mattar
   Cologne, 1981

187 Pendant
   Lutz-Albrecht Quambusch
   Lacquered bones, leather,
      pheasant feathers
   23 cm
   West Germany, 1982

188 Head jewelry
   Barbara Heinrich
   Polished steel, aluminum
   30 cm
   West Germany, 1981

189 Printing set
   Wendy Ramshaw
   Brass stamps, ink
   2 cm
   UK, 1982

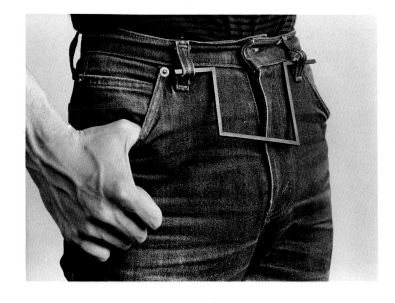

190 Neckpiece, armpiece
   Kai Chan
   Dogwood, thread
   22 cm, 10 cm
   Canada, 1983

191 Jeans piece
   Jan Wehrens
   Blue steel
   16 × 10.6 cm
   West Germany, 1982

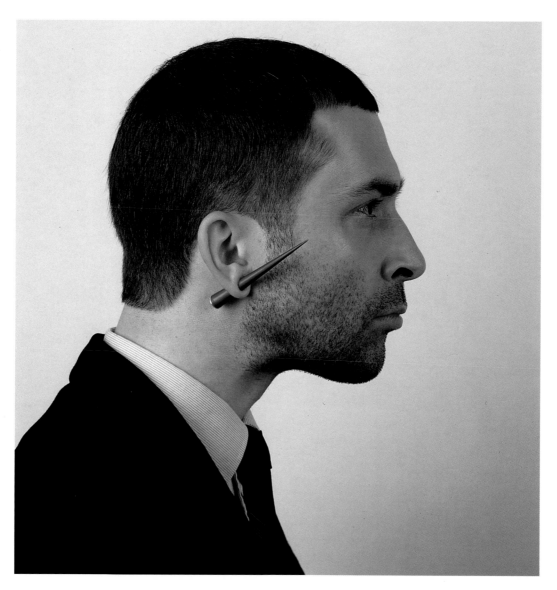

192 Blue Point
    Earpieces
    Wilhelm Mattar
    Aluminum, silver, steel
    9 cm
    West Germany, 1982

193 Earpieces
    Wilhelm Mattar
    Gold, steel
    7 cm
    West Germany, 1982

194, 195
German-Japanese Friendship
Earpieces
Wilhelm Mattar
Gold, steel
13 cm
West Germany, 1982

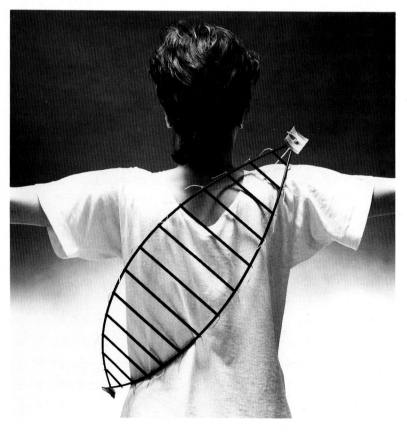

196 Ladder piece and
     balloon
    Pierre Degen
    Rubber, wood
    2 m, 60 cm d
    UK, 1983

197 Ladder piece
    Julia Manheim
    Plastic tubing
    60 cm
    UK, 1983

198 Neckpiece
    Marjorie Schick
    Painted wood
    60 cm h
    USA, 1983

Overleaf
199 Primary Orbits
    Neckpiece
    David Watkins
    Neoprene over steel
    39 cm d
    UK, 1983

INFORMATION

Biographies of makers

Galleries and Museums

Exhibitions

Publications

Index

BIOGRAPHIES OF MAKERS

Aleman, Jean-Paul b. France 1954. Self-taught textile designer. Exhibitions include *Jewelry Redefined*, London 1982.

Babetto, Giampaolo b. Italy 1947. Studied at the Instituto d'Arte, Padua; Academia di belle arti, Venice. Important exhibitions include Stedelijk Museum, Amsterdam 1977; Van Reekummuseum, Apeldoorn 1978; Tokyo Jewelry Triennale 1983.

Bakker, Gijs b. Holland 1942. Studied at the Instituut voor Kunstnijuerheidsonderwijs, Amsterdam. He has had a number of significant solo or two-person jewelry exhibitions with his wife, Emmy van Leersum. These two makers, both very influential, were especially important in the late 1960s and early 1970s. An early major joint exhibition was *Sculpture to Wear*, Amsterdam 1966 and London 1967. Bakker now works mainly, but not exclusively, as an industrial designer and among his design exhibitions *The Industrial Art of Gijs Bakker* (Crafts Council, London 1978) was important.

Bauer, Frank b. Germany 1942. Studied gold- and silversmithing, then design and architecture in Hamburg. His design and architectural interests are important influences on his jewelry – indeed, he also works in applied design. Currently living and working in Australia.

Becker, Friedrich b. Germany 1922. Studied at the Werkunstschule, Düsseldorf. Becker is respected for his excellent workmanship and his innovations with kinetic jewelry. He is an influential teacher and his own work is in most of the important European collections, such as the Worshipful Company of Goldsmiths, London, and the Schmuckmuseum, Pforzheim.

Bennett, James b. USA 1948. Studied in the department of Gold- and Silversmithing at State University College, New Paltz, New York. Has been apprenticed to Barry Merritt (goldsmith) and assistant to William Harper (enamellist). Now one of the USA's leading modern enamellists. Important group exhibitions include *Good As Gold*, Washington D.C. 1981 and USA tour.

Bischoff, Manfred b. West Germany 1947. Studied under Hermann Jünger in Munich. Bischoff's work is untypical of the younger West German jewelers in that it is freer in its composition than most and uses non-precious materials.

Boekhoudt, Onno b. Holland 1944. Studied at the Vakschool Schoonhoven and the Kunst und Werkschule, Pforzheim. Teaches at the Gerrit Rietveld Akademie, Amsterdam. Important exhibitions include *Schmuck International 1900–1980*, Vienna 1980; Galerie Ra, Amsterdam 1977, 1979, 1981 and 1983.

Brakman, Joke b. Holland 1946. Studied at the Gerrit Rietveld Akademie, Amsterdam. She is one of the leading 'reductivist' jewelers in Holland, placing great emphasis on the wearability of her work. Her jewelry has been widely exhibited and is in many public collections, including the Stedelijk Museum, Amsterdam.

Brink, Mecky van den b. Holland 1950. Studied textiles at the Gerrit Rietveld Akademie, Amsterdam. Developed her own textile jewelry in 1979 and, like several young designer-jewelers in Holland, has been impressed by the use of textiles and colour in the work of the English jeweler, Caroline Broadhead. Mecky van den Brink's work is in museum collections in

Arnhem and Amsterdam, and in the University of Amsterdam.

Broadhead, Caroline b. UK 1950. Studied at the Central School of Art, London. Her early work involved colouring ivory but she became interested in less restrictive materials. By 1977 she was producing bound-cotton necklaces and in 1978 she devised an influential design whereby a wearer pushed his or her hand or head through tufts of nylon held in place in a wood or silver frame. She was one of the first of the new jewelers in Europe to use textiles and her use of bright colour can be seen as a continuation of the pioneering work of Fritz Maierhofer and Claus Bury. She has exhibited widely and is represented in several important collections, including the Knapp Collection, New York (*The Jewelry Project*).

Bury, Claus b. West Germany 1946. Studied at Pforzheim as a goldsmith, but his major innovation was to combine gold and acrylics. In 1972 he shared the prize for the International Jewelry Competition at the Schmuckmuseum, Pforzheim. Following a highly successful contribution to a show at the Electrum Gallery, London (*Objects and Acrylic Jewelry*, 1972), Bury was invited to teach at the Royal College of Art, London. Later, at the Bezalel Academy of Art, Jerusalem, his work was experimental and sculptural. Although he was a major influence on modern jewelry throughout the 1970s, by the end of the decade he had decided to work solely as a sculptor – which he now does in the USA.

Cepka, Anton b. Czechoslovakia 1936. Studied in Bratislava and Prague and became a leading figure in modern jewelry in his country. He is a sculptor as well as a jeweler. For more examples of his work see the catalogue to *Schmuck International 1900–1980*, Vienna 1980.

Chan, Kai b. Hong Kong 1940, Canadian citizen. Studied at Chung Chei College, Chinese University of Hong Kong; Ontario College of Art. He is an interior designer, but his contributions to jewelry have been shown in *Jewelry Redefined*, London 1982; *Jewelry In Transition*, Toronto 1983; *Art by Design*, Canada House, London 1984.

Degen, Joël b. France 1941. Studied English at Montpelier University and did not become a jeweler until settling in the UK in 1965. He is a De Beers *Diamonds Today* prizewinner and is highly regarded as a craftsman, with work in several public collections including the Worshipful Company of Goldsmiths, London, and the National Gallery of Victoria, Australia. Not related to Pierre Degen.

Degen, Pierre b. Switzerland 1947. Studied jewelry at the Ecole d'Arts Appliqués, La Chaux-de-Fonds, Switzerland. Worked as a jewelry designer at Bucherer AG and as a technician in the jewelry department at the Central School of Art and Design, London; currently lecturer at Middlesex Polytechnic, London. He is regarded as one of the most radical of the new jewelers and his exhibition *Pierre Degen-New Work* (Crafts Council, London 1982) generated considerable argument. He has shown extensively throughout Europe.

Derrez, Paul b. Holland 1950. Studied goldsmithing but became known for jewelry which used non-precious materials and which was designed to be worn either by men or women. In 1976 he founded the highly influential Galerie Ra in Amsterdam. A frequent juror for exhibitions, he has his own work in the collection of the Stedelijk Museum, Amsterdam.

Didur, David b. Canada 1953. Studied in New York, Florence and Tokyo, as well as at Nova Scotia College of Art and Design. He has exhibited mainly in Canada, including *Jewelry In Transition*, Toronto 1983.

Dobler, George b. West Germany 1952. Studied goldsmithing in Pforzheim. Like Manfred Bischoff, George Dobler is unusual among younger West German jewelers in his preference for non-precious materials and a generally lighter interpretation of his craft. He had a solo exhibition at Galerie Ra, Amsterdam 1981; group exhibitions include *The Jewelry Project*, London 1983.

Dziuba, Gabriele b. West Germany 1951. Studied under Hermann Jünger, Munich. Important group exhibitions include *The Jewelry Project*, London 1983.

Ebendorf, Robert b. USA 1938. Studied at the University of Kansas. Professor of Art at the State University of New York. Work in public collections, including Schmuckmuseum, Pforzheim; Cooper-Hewitt Museum, New York; Twentieth Century Decorative Arts Collection, Metropolitan Museum of Art, New York.

Evans, James b. Canada 1952. Studied at Nova Scotia College of Art and Design. Evans is one of the young innovators in Canadian jewelry and potentially one of those likely to make a contribution to the new-jewelry movement of art-orientated work. He appears to take his cue from Europe rather than North America. Important exhibitions include *Jewelry In Transition*, Toronto 1983.

Fisch, Arline b. USA 1931. Studied at Skidmore College, New York; University of Illinois. She has had numerous solo exhibitions in the USA and UK and is well known for pioneering a technique in which strands of silver are knitted together, sometimes creating a lace effect. She is the author of *Textile Techniques in Metal* (1975) and a noted teacher.

Fok, Nora b. Hong Kong 1953. Studied Hong Kong Polytechnic; Brighton College of Art, UK. Group exhibitions include *The Jewelry Project*, London 1983; *Jewelry Redefined*, London 1982.

Grosse-Ruyken, Rita b. West Germany 1948. Studied in Munich (under Hermann Jünger) and Paris. She sees her work both as jewelry and as sculpture and, unlike most applied artists, tries to incorporate metaphor in it. Exhibits widely in West Germany and is usually represented in international group shows.

Harper, William b. USA 1944. Studied at Western Reserve University, Cleveland. Exhibited throughout USA and also in Europe. His catholic tastes in applied arts are reflected in the eclectic references in his work to a wide range of exotic and tribal cultures. Harper's work is held in several American public collections, including the American Craft Museum, New York; Metropolitan Museum of Art, New York.

Hees, Maria b. Holland 1948. Studied at Akademie voor Beeldende Kunsten, Arnhem. In the mid-to-late 1970s she began to treat jewelry as part of her industrial design activity, using manufactured materials and industrial components. She worked closely with Marja Staajes – both were pupils of Gijs Bakker.

Herbst, Marion b. Germany 1944. Studied at the Gerrit Rietveld Akademie, Amsterdam. A founder member of the B.O.E. group (1973) and instrumental in showing young Dutch jewelers an alternative to the reductivist De Stijl aesthetic favoured in the early 1970s. Exhibited extensively in Holland, UK, Belgium. Solo exhibitions include Galerie Ra, 1981. Major retrospective at the Van Reekummuseum, Apeldoorn 1982. Work in public collections, including Stedelijk Museum, Amsterdam.

Hermsen, Herman b. Holland 1953. Studied at the Akademie voor Beeldende Kunsten, Arnhem. Important group exhibitions include *Views on Jewelry, 1965–1982*, Amsterdam 1982; *Some Dutch Jewelry*, Bristol 1984.

Heron, Susanna b. UK 1949. Studied at the Central School of Art, London. First solo exhibition at Electrum Gallery, London 1972. A series of solo exhibitions since then have charted her development as a major influence in new jewelry in the UK and Holland. With her husband, photographer David Ward, she chose the works for *The Jewelry Project*, a collection of modern European jewelry (1980–83) for the New York collectors, Malcolm and Sue Knapp, first shown as an exhibition at the Crafts Council, London 1983. Her own work is in many public and private collections, including Crafts Council, London; Victoria and Albert Museum, London; Stedelijk Museum, Amsterdam. Now working as a sculptor.

Hess-Dahm, Johanna b. Switzerland 1947. Studied goldsmithing in Zürich. Solo exhibitions include Galerie Ra, Amsterdam 1982.

Hilbert, Therese b. Switzerland 1948. Studied in Zürich, and in Munich with Hermann Jünger. Has exhibited widely, including *The Jewelry Project*, London 1983.

Ho, Ron b. Hawaii 1937. Studied Education at the Pacific Lutheran University; University of Washington. He has travelled extensively in South America, Europe and the Orient and many of his works are assemblages using objects found on his travels. Exhibited widely throughout the USA.

Holder, Elisabeth b. West Germany 1950. Studied at the Staatliche Zeichenakademie, Hanau; Fachhochschule, Düsseldorf; Royal College of Art, London. Works in UK. She has lectured in Australia and her group exhibitions include *The Tenth Year*, Electrum Gallery, London 1981; *Tendenzen 1982*, Pforzheim; *Ring/Ringe*, at three locations in 1983: Aspects, London; Galerie Spectrum, Munich; Galerie Mattar, Cologne. Collections include Crafts Council, London; Schmuckmuseum, Pforzheim; Goldschmiedehaus, Hanau; Museum für Kunstgewerbe, Berlin.

Holdsworth, Annie b. Australia 1953. Studied at the Royal Melbourne Institute of Technology. Like others in her generation she is finding a style separate from the all-pervasive West European influences. She has exhibited quite widely and her work is in most state collections in Australia.

Honing, Willem b. Holland 1955. Studied at the Gerrit Rietveld Akademie, Amsterdam. Exhibitions include Galerie Ra, Amsterdam 1982.

Jünger, Hermann b. Germany 1928. Studied at the Staatliche Zeichenakademie, Hanau. Currently Professor of Goldsmithing at the Akademie der Bildenden Künste, Munich. Jünger's importance to modern jewelry is considerable and will become more so as his work becomes widely known in the rest of Europe and the USA. Although he is considered pre-eminent by West German modern jewelers and by jewelers all over the world who know of his work, he has had surprisingly few major exhibitions abroad. Many makers have learned – and borrowed – from his jewelry. He has taught many of the most interesting talents, such as Otto Künzli and Daniel Kruger, both of whom are radically different from each other, as well as from Jünger himself.

Karpyshin, Richard b. Canada 1955. Studied at the University of Manitoba School of Art; Nova Scotia College of Art and Design. Exhibited in *Jewelry In Transition*, Toronto 1983.

Kasaly, Svatopluk b. Czechoslovakia 1944. Studied at the Vocational School of Glassmaking, Zelenzy Brod School of Applied Arts. Important exhibitions include the *Tendenzen* biennial exhibitions at the Schmuckmuseum, Pforzheim; *Jewelry in Europe*, London 1975.

Knobel, Esther b. Poland 1949. Studied at the Bezalel Academy of Art, Jerusalem; Royal College of Art, London. The striking aspect of her work has been the combination of figuration and decorative abstract pattern. A very few of the pieces have been covertly political, but always the intention is to produce strong, amusing, decorative work that comes alive when worn. Represented in most important group exhibitions.

Koopman, Rena-Beatrice b. USA 1945. Studied at Vassar College, Poughkeepsie, New York, with additional studies in jewelry and sculpture in various institutions.

Kruger, Daniel b. South Africa 1951. Studied first as a graphic designer and then went to Munich under Hermann Jünger. Kruger's work is impressive not only for its technical virtuosity but also for its ever-changing imagery. It follows no single theory or aesthetic. He lives and works in Munich and has exhibited widely in West Germany; also in Galerie Ra, Amsterdam.

Künzli, Otto b. Switzerland 1948. Studied metalwork in Zürich, jewelry in Munich under Hermann Jünger. Although Künzli can be described as an anti-establishment jeweler, his work is better conceived and crafted than that description might suggest. Its cleverness rests in its ability to subvert conventional decorative jewelry while remaining in itself very attractive. He is one of the most able of the younger modern 'jewelers' and one of those most ill at ease with the values and traditions associated with jewelry. Important solo exhibitions include Schmuckmuseum, Pforzheim 1979; Galerie Ra, Amsterdam 1981; Deutsches Tapetenmuseum, Kassel 1983.

LaPlantz, David b. USA 1944. Studied metalsmithing at Cranbrook Academy of Art; also a major in art at the College of Education, Bowling Green State University. A hugely energetic jeweler. Works at great speed and is a frequent exhibitor – as well as a constant prizewinner. His students enjoy his teaching. Work in several collections, including the American Craft Museum, New York; Schmuckmuseum, Pforzheim.

Large, Edward de b. UK 1945. Studied at Camberwell School of Art; Royal College of Art, London. Meticulous craftsman, who did much pioneering work with anodizing titanium.

Lechtzin, Stanley b. USA 1936. Studied at Cranbrook Academy of Art; Wayne State University. Professor of Design at Tyler School of Art, Philadelphia, since 1962. An important figure in the development of modern American jewelry. Has exhibited widely in USA and also in Europe.

Leersum, Emmy van b. Holland 1930. Studied at the Instituut voor Kunstnijuerheidsonderwijs, Amsterdam. With her husband Gijs Bakker, she is the most important figure in the recent history of modern jewelry in Holland, though her pioneering, radical and innovative work really falls in the period of the mid-1960s to the mid-1970s. Since then several other figures, with different ideas, have emerged in Holland. She helped to bring together aspects of sculpture, minimalist art and ornament. Exhibited extensively which, together with teaching and study tours throughout Western Europe and the USA, made the Van Leersum/Bakker partnership especially influential. Public collections include Stedelijk Museum, Amsterdam; Victoria and Albert Museum, London.

Mahlow, Beatrix b. West Germany 1957. Studied at the Hochschule der Künste, Berlin; Middlesex Polytechnic, London. Work in the Cleveland County Museum, UK.

Maierhofer, Fritz b. Austria 1941. Shown extensively in Europe and was one of the prominent new jewelers of the early and mid-1970s, though his work continues to develop. An influential teacher, represented in various collections, including Schmuckmuseum, Pforzheim.

Makigawa, Carlier b. Australia 1952. Studied at Claremont and Freemantle Technical College; Western Australian Institute of Technology. International and touring exhibitions include *Australian Jewelry*, toured Europe 1982–83; *Jewelry Redefined*, London 1982.

Manheim, Julia b. UK 1949. Studied Central School of Art, London. One of a group – the others included Caroline Broadhead and Susanna Heron – that emerged from the Central School and that has been in the forefront of new jewelry in the UK for the last ten years. Work in public collections, including Crafts Council, London; Victoria and Albert Museum, London; National Gallery of Victoria, Australia.

Martinazzi, Bruno b. Italy 1923. Sculptor and jeweler. Studied first as an industrial chemist, then at the State School of Art, Florence. Important group exhibitions include *Schmuck International 1900–1980*, Vienna 1980; *Jewelry in Europe*, London 1975.

Mattar, Wilhelm T. b. West Germany 1946. Studied jewelry and design at Pforzheim. Opened Galerie Mattar in Cologne, which he owns and runs, in 1979. Has shown his own work in Austria, Belgium, Japan, West Germany and UK. Important group exhibitions include *Schmuck International 1900–1980*, Vienna 1980; *International Jewelry Art Exhibition*, Tokyo 1983.

Mawdsley, Richard b. USA 1945. One of the most interesting of the younger American jewelers because he has channelled his expert craftsmanship into wholly idiosyncratic styles which have very little to do with modern fine – or applied – art ideas, yet are, none the less, contemporary objects. Work in public collections, including the National Museum of American Art, Smithsonian Institution, Washington D.C.

Metcalf, Bruce b. USA 1949. Studied at Syracuse University and then Tyler School of Art, Philadelphia. Currently Professor of Jewelry/Metals at Kent State University, Ohio. Metcalf is a jeweler, craftsman and sculptor. His work, though clearly quite different to that of Richard Mawdsley, is equally idiosyncratic – even taking into account the diverse range of American decorative art. There is no European counterpart to Metcalf in jewelry, though some of the younger British ornamentalist sculptors would find a common chord. Solo exhibitions include the Heller Gallery, New York 1981 and 1984. For further information about his work, see *Metalsmith* magazine, Autumn 1982.

Nele, E.R. b. West Germany. Studied at the Central School of Art, London 1950–55. Has exhibited widely in Europe and also participated in international exhibitions such as the *1st International Exhibition of Modern Jewelry*, London 1961, and *Schmuck International, 1900–1980*, Vienna 1980.

Niczewski, Peter b. UK 1948. Studied graphics at the Chelsea School of Art, London. Exhibitions include *Jewelry Redefined*, London 1982. Work shown in Galerie Ra, Amsterdam; Aspects, London.

Ommen, Joke van b. Holland 1948. Studied art history and architecture; private student of goldsmiths Erika Leitner and Peter Skubic. Currently teaching in the USA; the 'Dutch style' of her work has become modified into a noticeably American idiom. Exhibitions include *Schmuck International, 1900–1980*, Vienna 1980; *Jewelry Redefined*, London 1982; *Good As Gold*, Washington D.C. 1981 and USA tour.

Paley, Albert R., Jr. b. USA 1944. Studied sculpture at Tyler School of Art, Temple University, Philadelphia. Exhibited in major international exhibitions of jewelry, but is now an internationally acclaimed blacksmith working on architectural commissions. Work is in many collections, including the Renwick Gallery, Washington D.C.

Petry, Michael b. USA 1960. Studied art and mathematics, Rice University, Houston, Texas. Multimedia performance artist.

Planteydt, Annelies b. Holland 1956. Studied at the Gerrit Rietveld Akademie, Amsterdam. Work shown in Galerie Cada, Munich; Galerie Ra, Amsterdam.

Poston, David b. USSR 1948, UK citizen. Studied at Hornsey College of Art and Design, London. Exhibited in Europe and Australia. One of the first jewelers to use textiles in his work. Represented in Crafts Council Collection, London.

Quigley, Robin L. b. USA 1947. Studied at Tyler School of Art, Temple University, Philadelphia; Rhode Island School of Design. Important solo exhibitions include the Helen Drutt Gallery, Philadelphia, 1978 and 1981. Shows also at Galerie Ra, Amsterdam. Work in collections including Tyler School of Art; the Helen Drutt Gallery.

Ramshaw, Wendy b. UK 1939. Trained in illustration and fabric design; self-taught jeweler. Her collections of rings, often grouped together on lathe-turned miniature acrylic minarets, created a lot of interest in modern jewelry circles in the early 1970s. The bulk of her work continues to be well crafted in precious metals, but recently she has experimented with performances and has also produced, with her husband, David Watkins, a book of cut-out paper jewelry. She has exhibited widely and frequently all over the world and has work in many collections, including Victoria and Albert Museum, London; Schmuckmuseum, Pforzheim.

Reiling, Reinhold b. Germany 1922, d. 1983. A highly influential jeweler, assured of an important place in the history of 20th-century European jewelry. It goes without saying that, as a leading West German jeweler, his craftsmanship was superb, but so too was his design sense. His most recent solo exhibition was at the Schmuckmuseum, Pforzheim 1982 – and his work is in the Schmuckmuseum's collection.

Rezac, Susan b. Czechoslovakia 1953, Swiss citizen. Studied sculpture at the Rhode Island School of Design, USA. Shows with Helen Drutt Gallery, USA.

Rössle, Annette b. West Germany 1951. Studied under Hermann Jünger. Has exhibited in West Germany, but now owns and runs the Galerie Cada, Munich.

Rothmann, Gerd b. Germany 1941. Studied at the Staatliche Zeichenakademie, Hanau. Worked in Hermann Jünger's studio in 1966. Several solo and international group exhibitions, including some early group shows of importance (e.g. with Claus Bury and Fritz Maierhofer at Electrum, London 1972). One of the first jewelers to use acrylics. Continues link with Electrum (e.g. innovative body-works exhibition there in 1982). Work included in various collections, including Schmuckmuseum, Pforzheim.

Schick, Marjorie b. USA 1941. Studied at the University of Wisconsin; Indiana University; Sir John Cass School, London. A very innovative maker – and her work of the last twenty years gives the lie to the idea that all the radical work of recent decades has been European. Shows with Galerie Ra, Amsterdam; Aspects Gallery, London.

Scott, Ann b. USA 1959. Studied at Moore College of Art, Philadelphia. Group exhibitions include Helen Drutt Gallery, Philadelphia.

Selkirk, David b. Australia 1954. Studied at Western Australian Institute of Technology. Exhibited in numerous group shows in Australia. Exhibited in *Jewelry Redefined*, London 1982; *Australian Jewelry*, Tokyo 1983.

Sharlin, Miriam b. USA 1952. Studied at Bennington College, Bennington, Vermont; State University of New York, New Paltz, New York. A meticulous craftswoman whose work has been influenced by West German goldsmiths. She has had several solo exhibitions in the USA and West Germany, as well as being represented in most of the important international group exhibitions. Her work can be seen in the Schmuckmuseum, Pforzheim.

Shirk, Helen b. USA 1942. Studied at Skidmore College, New York; Kunsthaandvaerkerskolen, Copenhagen; Indiana University. Currently Professor of Art, San Diego State University. Exhibitions include *Tendenzen*, Pforzheim 1982; *Good As Gold*, Washington D.C. 1981 and USA tour; *Black Jewelry*, Oxford 1981. Work in public collections, including Indiana University Fine Arts Museum; University of Texas.

Skal, Hubertus von b. Czechoslovakia 1942, lives in Munich. Studied at the Akademie der Bildenden Künste, Munich. Exhibited widely in Europe and work shown in the USA. Has always been highly respected by fellow jewelers even when, as in the late 1970s, his fine workmanship in precious materials was outside the mainstream of contemporary jewelry. Recent international group shows include *Schmuck International 1900–1980*, Vienna 1980; *Tendenzen*, Pforzheim 1982.

Spiller, Eric b. UK 1946. Studied at the Central School of Art, London. His work is among the 'quietest' of that produced by the new innovative jewelers – very well made, precisely designed. Exhibited in Europe, USA, Australia. Work in public collections, including Crafts Council, London; the Worshipful Company of Goldsmiths, London.

Tisdale, David b. USA 1956. Studied design at the University of California; San Diego State University. Exhibited widely in California and abroad, including *Four American Jewelers*, Vienna 1983. Work shown at Galerie Ra, Amsterdam.

Watkins, David b. UK 1940. Studied sculpture at the University of Reading. Jazz musician. Exhibited widely in Europe, USA and Australia. His work over the last ten years presents one of the most consistent catalogues of thoughtful design and development in new jewelry. Work in public collections, including the Crafts Council, London; Worshipful Company of Goldsmiths, London.

Wehrens, Jan b. Holland 1945. Studied in Holland and West Germany, and now works in Munich. His work is closely associated with clothing – making allusions to buckles or epaulettes, for example – but combined with the decorative aspect is a hard, almost 'militaristic' image.

Woell, Fred b. USA 1934. Studied at the University of Illinois; University of Wisconsin; Cranbrook Academy of Art. An influential figure in American jewelry and known for his early satirical pieces. Work in public collections, including the American Craft Museum, New York; Helen Drutt Gallery, Philadelphia. Widely exhibited throughout the USA and a noted teacher and lecturer.

Wolf, Lam de b. Holland 1949. Studied textiles at the Gerrit Rietveld Akademie, Amsterdam. Her textile constructions and 'garments' are almost theatrical and, if not conventional jewelry, are certainly in the category of body ornament. In a curious way, she ventures into the anti-Modernist style of ornament that is finding favour with younger interior and fashion designers in Western Europe. Her work has been exhibited widely in Holland and Britain and is included in the collection of Mr and Mrs Knapp, New York.

GALLERIES AND MUSEUMS

Specialist, independent gallery directors have been crucial in the development of new art-jewelry. Such directors have had to be especially adventurous because the audience and the market for innovative work is still young. Yet independent galleries are succeeding, as well as surviving, and their role is important even in countries such as Britain and America where there are well-established public institutions supporting the crafts. In practice the independent galleries have been prepared to risk first showings of new talent, while the subsidized gallery directors usually need to have an eye on the demands of those who represent the interests of trustees or taxpayers.

The difference between a shop and a gallery is more than a difference of degree. A shop may well sell good work, but a gallery tries to develop a point of view. In a way a gallery is like a very good critic – you may not always agree with the stance or the conclusion but you can trust them because a policy and a consistent philosophy has been developed.

However, the subsidized galleries and museums have also become important, partly because – when they deal with jewelry – they can afford to be singleminded and don't have to compromise to make money (none but the most rigorous of the independent galleries specialize wholly in innovative art-jewelry). Equally, public institutions have the resources for good presentation and scholarship through well-researched, well-put-together leaflets and catalogues. A wider public is also reached through better, more professional promotional facilities.

There is some argument – it has been quite acrimonious in Britain, which has a substantial support system for art, craft, design and film – as to whether or not state subsidies encourage makers to forget the interests of the buying public. The criticism has been that by being provided with grants and exhibitions (which may lead to teaching posts in art schools) the makers have had very little need to sell their work: their work, their 'art', has therefore become introspective and of interest to fellow makers but not to others. There is some truth in this argument, but none the less the partnership between the state and independent galleries is encouraging a wider audience of informed people wanting and willing to buy jewelry which they might first have become aware of through the subsidized sector. New jewelry needs the vigour of the independent galleries to discover talent and sell it, while the public sector is required to consolidate reputations and maintain quality.

Among the key modern jewelry galleries Paul Derrez's *Galerie Ra* is one of the most important influences on jewelry in Holland and Britain. Galerie Ra's work has also prompted strong interest among connoisseurs elsewhere in Europe and in the United States. Its particular interpretation of modernism, with an emphasis upon non-precious jewelry that rejects the notion that jewelry must always declare status and position, runs counter to certain strong characteristics in West German, Austrian and American work. It is nevertheless true that Galerie Ra shows a wide range of jewelers.

Galleries are made by the people who run them and in Britain modern jewelry has been much helped by individuals, including Graham Hughes (who for a long time worked for the Worshipful Company of Goldsmiths, London); Ralph Turner and Barbara Cartlidge. In 1971, for example, Barbara Cartlidge and Ralph Turner founded the *Electrum Gallery* in London. The early 1970s saw a number of very important exhibitions at Electrum, with several major shows of European jewelers across a spectrum from Emmy van Leersum and Gijs Bakker to Hubertus von Skal. Ralph Turner left to become Head of Exhibitions at the Crafts Council, London, and Barbara Cartlidge continues to run Electrum with a stable of makers that includes Wendy

Ramshaw and Frank Bauer. Currently, the gallery in London seeking to rival Galerie Ra's reputation for intelligent, quality design is *Aspects*, founded in 1982 by Sharon Plant. Aspects is aiming for a European rather than simply a British voice and is also spreading its design interests into other areas, such as textiles and furniture.

In the United States of America the *Helen Drutt Gallery*, Philadelphia, is of much importance because it has shown many hitherto unknown makers from both Europe and the USA. Helen Drutt believes it is essential that a gallery should develop a point of view, and that the director should act as an editor, even a tastemaker. Her attitude to the relationship between fashion and jewelry, however, is not espoused by some of the other gallery owners in America dealing in modern jewelry. In an interesting round up of American gallery directors' views (*Metalsmith* magazine, Winter 1984), several directors agreed with Robert Lee Morris, director of *Art Wear*, New York, when he said: 'It is good to be influenced by fashion trends in order to stay current and not repeat what has already been done.' Helen Drutt, like Paul Derrez or Wilhelm Mattar of *Galerie Mattar* in Cologne, West Germany, concentrates on longer-term developments in aesthetics. But, of course, the fashion aspect of new jewelry is important because much of the new jewelry plays up to fashion-conscious, as well as design-conscious, people. There can be no hard-and-fast 'ideologies' in any of the decorative arts, and certainly not in jewelry.

The independent galleries and public museums listed below reflect the balance of entrepreneurial innovation and establishment endorsement outlined above. This list is by no means exhaustive, but it does present a good range of reliable, high-quality galleries and museums.

Australia
Art Gallery of South Australia, North Terrace, Adelaide 5000, South Australia
The Western Australian Art Gallery, Beaufort Street, Perth 6000, Western Australia
National Gallery of Victoria, Victoria Arts Centre, 180 St Kilda Road, Melbourne 3000, Victoria

These are state-assisted galleries, building collections of new Australian, European and American work.

Austria
Galerie am Graben, Graben 7, A-1010 Vienna
Galerie V & V, Lindengasse 5, A-1070 Vienna

Both galleries have lively modern exhibitions. Galerie am Graben is the longer established of the two, with a particular historical strength in Art Nouveau.

Belgium
Galerie Neon, 19 Rue Defacqz, 1050 Brussels

An adventurous and innovative gallery run by new jeweler Bernard François.

Canada
Prime Canadian Crafts, 229 Queen Street W, Toronto

Holland
Beeld en Aambeeld, Walstraat 33, 7511 GE Enschede
Den Bosch, Gemeente Museum, Arnhem
Flora Design, Grote Berg 1A, Eindhoven
Galerie De Sluis, Sluiskant 24, 2265 AB Leidschendam
Galerie Eewal, Eewal 84, 8911 GV Leeuwarden
Galerie Het Kapelhuis, Krankeledenstraat 11, Amersfoort
Galerie Marzee, Lange Hezelstraat 19, 6511 CA Nÿmegen
Galerie Nouvelles Images, Westeinde 22, 2512 HD Den Haag
Galerie Ra, Vijzelstraat 80, 1017 HL Amsterdam
Galerie Serafÿn, Minrebroederstraat 1, Utrecht
Stedelijk Museum, Paulus Porterstraat 13, 5082 Amsterdam
The Van Reekummuseum, Koninginnelaan 9, 7315 BJ Apeldoorn

Galerie Ra and Galerie Het Kapelhuis are independent galleries showing top quality new jewelry. The various museums are building important collections of modern jewelry, with an emphasis upon European work.

Switzerland
Byou Terrible, Zollikerstrasse 14, 8008 Zürich
Galleria Cubo, Via Maraini 27, CH 6900 Lugano
Galerie Michele Zeller, Kramgasse 20, 3011 Bern

UK
Anatol Orient, 28 Shelton Street, London WC2
Argenta, 82 Fulham Road, London SW3

Argosy Gallery and Bookshop, 2 Abbey Green, Bath BA1, Avon

Aspects Gallery, 3–5 Whitfield Street, London W1

Barclaycraft, 7 East Street, Brighton, Sussex

British Crafts Centre, 43 Earlham Street, London WC2

The Chestnut Gallery, High Street, Bourton-on-the-Water, Gloucestershire

Cleveland Crafts Centre, 57 Gilkes Street, Middlesbrough, Cleveland

Crafts Centre & Design Gallery, Leeds City Art Gallery, The Headrow, Leeds, West Yorkshire

Craft Centre, Royal Exchange Theatre, St Ann's Square, Manchester

Crafts Council Gallery, 12 Waterloo Place, London SW1

Dartington Craft Shop, Ciderpress Gallery, Shinners Bridge, Dartington, Totnes, Devon

Electrum Gallery, 21 South Molton Street, London W1

Facets, 22 New Quebec Street, London W1

Focus Gallery, 108 Derby Road, Nottingham

James Rossiter, 38–41 Broad Street, Bath, Avon

Katherine House Gallery, The Parade, Marlborough, Wiltshire

Long Street Gallery, 50 Long Street, Tetbury, Gloucestershire

The Midland Group Shop, 24–32 Carlton Street, Nottingham

New Ashgate Gallery, Downing Street, Farnham, Surrey

New Craftsman, 24 Fore Street, St Ives, Cornwall

Oxford Gallery, 23 High Street, Oxford

Primavera, 10 King's Parade, Cambridge

The Scotish Crafts Centre, 140 Cannongate, Royal Mile, Edinburgh

Victoria and Albert Museum, South Kensington, London SW7

Worshipful Company of Goldsmiths, Goldsmiths Hall, Foster Lane, London EC2

Aspects and Electrum are the two key independent commercial galleries in London. The British Crafts Centre, independently minded although heavily subsidized by the Crafts Council, has an excellent range of work. The Victoria and Albert Museum is Britain's museum of the decorative arts; new jewelry is a small but serious part of the institution's interest. The Worshipful Company of Goldsmiths has a history going back 800 years, but has an important collection of modern jewelry.

USA

The American Craft Museum, 73 W 45th Street, New York, NY 10019

Art Wear, 409 West Broadway, New York, NY 10013

Betsy Rosenfield Gallery, 212 W. Superior, Chicago, IL 60610

Blue Streak Gallery, Inc, 1723 Delaware Avenue, Wilmington, DE 19806

Byzantium, 105 Thompson Street, New York, NY 10012

Concepts, 6th & Mission Street, Carmel, CA 93921

Contemporary Artisans Gallery, 530 Bush Street, San Francisco, CA 94108

Contemporary Crafts, 3934 S.W. Corbett Avenue, Portland, OR 97201

Convergence, 484 Broome Street, New York, NY 10013

Cooper-Hewitt Museum of Decorative Arts and Design, Smithsonian Institution, 9 E. 90th Street, New York, NY 10019

Craftsman's Gallery, 16 Chase Road, Scarsdale, NY 10583

Detail, 204 Spring Street, New York, NY 10012

Elizabeth Fortner Gallery, 1114 State Street, Studio 9-La Arcada Court, Santa Barbara, CA 93101

Etienne, 20 Main Street, Camden, ME 04843

Freehand, 8413 W. 3rd Street, Los Angeles, CA 90048

Gallery Eight, 7464 Girard Avenue, La Jolla, CA 92037

Gallery 10, 21 Greenwich Avenue, New York, NY 10014

Gayle Willson Gallery, 42b Jobs Lane, Southampton, NY 11968

Graham Gallery, 908 Prospect St, La Jolla, CA 92037

Handcrafters Gallery, 44 Exchange Street, Portland, ME 04101

Helen Drutt Gallery, 1721 Walnut Street, Philadelphia, PA 19103

Jackie Chalkley Gallery, 3301 New Mexico Avenue N.W., Washington, D.C. 20016

Maple Hill Gallery, 367 Fore Street, Portland, ME 04101

Merritt Gallery, 800 Powers Building, Rochester, NY 14614

Mindscape, 1521 Sherman Avenue, Evanston, IL 60201

Perception Galleries, 1724 Bissonnet, Houston, TX 77005

Plum Gallery, 3762 Howard Avenue, Kensington, MD 20895

Renwick Gallery of the National Museum of American Art (Smithsonian Institution), Pennsylvania Avenue at 17th Street N.W., Washington, D.C. 20560

Sheila Nussbaum Gallery, 358 Millburn Avenue, Millburn, NJ 07041

A Singular Place, 2718 Main Street, Santa Monica, CA 90405

Spring Street Enamels Gallery, 171 Spring Street, New York, NY 10012

Swan Galleries, 8433 Germantown Avenue, Philadelphia, PA 19118

Ten Arrow, Ten Arrow Street, Cambridge, MA 02138

V O Galerie – Contemporary Jewelry, 2000 Pennsylvania Avenue, Washington, D.C. 20006

Westminster Gallery, 132A Newbury Street, Boston, MA 02116

Whichcraft, 52 Vose Avenue, South Orange, NJ 07079

There are a great many craft shops, galleries, museums and public collections throughout the USA and interested viewers are urged to contact such organizations as the American Craft Council, 401 Park Avenue South, New York, NY 10016 or the Society of North American Goldsmiths, University of South Illinois, Carbondale, Illinois. The Renwick Gallery is especially important since it is intended to function as a national gallery for American design and the decorative arts. The American Craft Museum has regular exhibitions, some of which are given to national or foreign new jewelry exhibitions.

West Germany

Atelier AKUT, Südstrasse 10, 4150 Krefeld

D'OR, Herbartgang 11, 2900 Oldenburg

Galerie Cada, Hans-Sachs-Strasse 11, D-8000 Munich 5

Galerie Feinschmiede, Windscheidstrasse 24, 1000 Berlin 12

Galerie Mattar, Lüttiger Strasse 46, 5 Cologne 1

Galerie Orferre, Bastionstrasse 31, 4000 Düsseldorf

Galerie Rehklau, Alte Gasse 11, 89001 Augsburg

Galerie Spectrum, Türkenstrasse 97, D-8000 Munich 40

Galerie Ventil, Kirchenstrasse 69, D-8000 Munich 80

The Goldschmiedehaus, Altstadter Markt 6, Hanau am Main 645

The Hessiches Landesmuseum, Friedenplatz, 61 Darmstadt

Museum für Kunst und Gewerbe, 1 Steintorplatz, Hamburg 2

Schmuckmuseum Pforzheim im Reuchlinhaus, Jahnstrasse 42, Pforzheim 753

Sternthaler, Ermekeilstrasse 16, 5300 Bonn 1

Werkstattgalerie, Meierottostrasse 1, 1000 Berlin 15

Since it is the only museum of jewelry, the Schmuckmuseum at Pforzheim is important, as are its biennial *Tendenzen* exhibitions. The smaller, commercial galleries, such as Cada, Spectrum and Mattar, show very good modern work by jewelers from all over Europe and the USA. The Museum für Kunst und Gewerbe contains a variety of twentieth-century work, as does the Hessiches Landesmuseum (with its noted Art Nouveau collection) which also stages international exhibitions of modern jewelry.

EXHIBITIONS

A selected list of important exhibitions with catalogues

1961 *1st International Exhibition of Modern Jewelry*, Worshipful Company of Goldsmiths, London

1963 *Modern British Jewelry*, Worshipful Company of Goldsmiths, London

1965 *Internationale Ausstellung Schmuck*, Hessisches Landesmuseum, Darmstadt, West Germany

1966 Friedrich Becker, Worshipful Company of Goldsmiths, London

1967 *Tendenzen*, Schmuckmuseum, Pforzheim, West Germany – first of an international biennial series still continuing

1969 *Objects to Wear* (Van Leersum, Bakker, Van Beek, Van der Bosch, Lameris), Van Abbemuseum, Eindhoven, Holland; then USA tour

1970 *International Exhibition of Jewelry*, Tokyo – first of an international triennial series still continuing

1970 Gerda Flöckinger, Victoria and Albert Museum, London

1972 *Sieraad 1900–1972*, Zonnehof Museum, Amersfoort, Holland

1972 Rüdiger Lorenzen, Schmuckmuseum, Pforzheim, West Germany

1973 *British Jewelry*, Electrum Gallery, London; then Holland tour

1973 *The Craftsman's Art*, Crafts Advisory Committee (now Crafts Council), London

1974 Claus Bury, Schmuckmuseum, Pforzheim, West Germany

1974 *Schmuck Aus Stahl*, International Symposium, Vienna

1975 *On Tour – Ten British Jewelers*, Crafts Council, London. Toured West Germany and Australia

1975 *Contemporary Crafts of America*. Toured USA

1975 *Jewelry in Europe*, Victoria and Albert Museum, London; then UK tour

1976 *Jewelry of Margaret de Patta*, Oakland, California, USA

1976 *Loot*, Worshipful Company of Goldsmiths, London – first of an annual series still continuing

1978 Claus Bury, Hermann Jünger, Gerd Rothmann, Hessiches Landesmuseum, Darmstadt, West Germany

1979 Otto Künzli, Schmuckmuseum, Pforzheim, West Germany

1980 *Schmuck International 1900–1980*, Kunstler Osterreiche, Vienna

1980 Emmy van Leersum Retrospective, Stedelijk Museum, Amsterdam

1980 Susanna Heron, *Bodywork*, Crafts Council, London

1981 Caroline Broadhead, Arnolfini Gallery, Bristol, UK

1981 Hermann Jünger, Galerie am Graben, Vienna

1981 *Ready Made*, Galerie Mattar, Cologne, West Germany

1981 *Beyond Tradition*, American Craft Museum, New York

1981 *Good as Gold*, Renwick Gallery, Smithsonian Institution, Washington D.C.; then USA tour

1982 *Jewelry Redefined*, International Exhibition, British Crafts Centre, London; then European tour

1982 Pierre Degen, *New Work*, Crafts Council, London

1982 Fritz Maierhofer, Galerie am Graben, Vienna

1982 *Views on Jewelry 1965–1982*, Stedelijk Museum, Amsterdam

1982 Reinhold Reiling, Schmuckmuseum, Pforzheim, West Germany

1983 Otto Künzli, Deutsches Tapetenmuseum, Kassel, West Germany

1983 *The Jewelery Project* (Knapp Collection), Crafts Council, London – the private collection of Mr and Mrs Knapp, New York

1983 *New Departures in British Jewelry*, American Craft Museum, New York; then USA tour

1984 Daniel Kruger, Schmuckmuseum, Pforzheim, West Germany

1984 *Some Dutch Jewelry*, Arnolfini Gallery, Bristol, UK

PUBLICATIONS

Magazines

Each of these magazines gives some coverage to modern jewelry and each has been chosen for the high standard of both its editorial and illustrative content.

American Craft, 401 Park Avenue South, New York, NY 10016, USA

Arts Review, 16 St James's Gardens, London W11, UK

Bÿvoorbeeld, Keizersgracht 135, 1015 CK Amsterdam, Holland

Craft Australia, 100 George Street, The Rocks, Sydney, NSW 2000, Australia

Crafts, Crafts Council, 8 Waterloo Place, London SW1Y 4AU, UK

Form & Function, Finnish Society of Craft and Design, Erottajankatu 15–17, A502, 00130, Helsinki 13, Finland

Gold und Silber und Schmuck, Konradin-Verlag, D 7022 Leinfelden bei Stuttgart, West Germany

Goldschmiede Zeitung, Rühle-Diebener-Verlag, Postfach 450, 7000 Stuttgart 70, West Germany

Items, POB 3282, 2601 DG Delft, Holland

Jewelry Journal, 3-44-7 Honeo, Bunkyo Ku, Tokyo, Japan

Kunst & Handwerk, Postfach 8120, D4000 Düsseldorf 1, West Germany

Metalsmith, 2849 St Ann Drive, Green Bay, W1 54301, USA

Ornament, POB 35029, Los Angeles, CA 90035-0029, USA

Outline, Stichting Cosa, Oude Delft 1836, Delft, Holland

Books

There are many, many books devoted to do-it-yourself jewelry and very few devoted to giving any form of critical assessment of new jewelry. We offer two professional books on methods and technique, especially recommending Oppi Untracht's for its detailed, all-embracing character. The rest should interest those who find this book interesting.

Fisch, Arline, *Textile Techniques in Metal* (Van Nostrand Reinhold, New York, 1975)

Hinks, Peter, *Twentieth-century British Jewelry 1900–1980* (Faber & Faber, London, 1983; Faber & Faber Inc, Winchester Mass., 1983)

Hughes, Graham, *Modern Jewelry* (Studio Vista, London, 1963; Crown, New York, 1963)

Hughes, Graham, *The Art of Jewelry* (Studio Vista, London, 1972)

Reiling, Reinhold, *Goldschmiedekunst* (Verlag Ernst Wasmuth, Tübingen, 1978)

Schollmayer, Karl, *Neuer Schmuck* (Verlag Ernst Wasmuth, Tübingen, 1974)

Turner, Ralph, *Contemporary Jewelry: A Critical Assessment 1945–1975* (Studio Vista, London, 1976; Van Nostrand Reinhold, New York, 1976)

Untracht, Oppi, *Jewelry Concepts and Technology* (Doubleday, New York, 1982; Robert Hale, London, 1982)

Ward, Anne, and others, *The Ring: From Antiquity to the Twentieth Century* (Thames and Hudson, London, 1981)

Wilcox, David, *Body Jewelry* (Henry Regnery, Chicago, 1973; Pitman, London, 1973)

INDEX

Numerals in italics refer to plate numbers